Best of Enemi

James Graham

Inspired by the documentary by
Morgan Neville and Robert Gordon

methuen | drama

LONDON • NEW YORK • OXFORD • NEW DELHI • SYDNEY

METHUEN DRAMA

Bloomsbury Publishing Plc

50 Bedford Square, London, WC1B 3DP, UK

1385 Broadway, New York, NY 10018, USA

29 Earlsfort Terrace, Dublin 2, Ireland

BLOOMSBURY, METHUEN DRAMA and the Methuen Drama logo
are trademarks of Bloomsbury Publishing Plc

First published in Great Britain 2021

This edition published 2022

Cover design: AKA

Photography: Johan Persson

A catalogue record for this book is available from the British Library.

A catalog record for this book is available from the Library of Congress.

ISBN: PB: 978-1-3503-8126-1
ePDF: 978-1-3503-8128-5
eBook: 978-1-3503-8127-8

Series: Modern Plays

Typeset by Newgen KnowledgeWorks Pvt. Ltd., Chennai, India
Printed and bound in Great Britain

To find out more about our authors and books visit
www.bloomsbury.com and sign up for our newsletters.

Best of Enemies transferred to London's West End, opening at the Noël Coward Theatre on 14 November 2022 with the following cast and creative team.

Cast

David Harewood   William F. Buckley Jr
Zachary Quinto   Gore Vidal

Deborah Alli   Aretha Franklin, Patty the
                           Party Guest, Brooke Gladstone
David Boyle   Ensemble
Lincoln Conway   Ensemble
Emilio Doorgasingh   William Sheehan, Chet Huntley,
                           Howard Austen
Vivienne Ekwulugo   Ensemble
Clare Foster   Patricia Buckley
Tom Godwin   Frank Meyer, Andy Warhol,
                           Bobby Kennedy, David Brinkley,
                           Enoch Powell
John Hodgkinson   Howard K. Smith, Mayor Daley
Jamie Hogarth   Ensemble
Syrus Lowe   James Baldwin, George Merlis,
                           Martin Luther King Jr
Kevin McMonagle   Elmer Lower, Walter Cronkite
Sam Otto   Tariq Ali, Matt
Saaj Raja   Ensemble

Understudies

David Boyle   Elmer Lower, Walter Cronkite,
                           Howard K. Smith, Mayor Daley
Lincoln Conway   William F. Buckley Jr, James
                           Baldwin, George Merlis,
                           Martin Luther King Jr
Vivienne Ekwulugo   Patricia Buckley, Aretha Franklin,
                           Patty the Party Guest,
                           Brooke Gladstone

Jamie Hogarth	Gore Vidal, Frank Meyer, Andy Warhol, Bobby Kennedy, David Brinkley
Saaj Raja	Tariq Ali, Matt, William Sheehan, Chet Huntley, Howard Austen

Creative Team

Jeremy Herrin	Director
Bunny Christie	Designer
Jack Knowles	Lighting Designer
Tom Gibbons	Sound Designer
Max Spielbichler	Video Designer
Benjamin Kwasi Burrell	Composer
Shelley Maxwell	Movement Director
Charlotte Sutton CDG	UK Casting Director
Jim Carnahan CSA	US Casting Director
Annie Kershaw	Associate Director
Hazel Holder	Voice and Dialect

SECOND
HALF
PRODUCTIONS

Second Half Productions is an entertainment company founded by Jeremy Herrin, Alan Stacey and Rob O'Rahilly in 2021 to generate innovative productions for stage and screen.

By commissioning world-leading artists to create new work and by breathing new life into classic stories, we invigorate audiences in London, the UK and beyond. Our ambition is to produce entertainment that engages the broadest range of people and in doing so creates meaningful opportunities for those who are currently underrepresented in the sector. We're a company of creatives, producers and general managers and we're driven and inspired by the artists that we work with.

Our inaugural production, *The Glass Menagerie,* opened at the Duke of York's Theatre in May 2022.

Co-Founders & Directors	**Jeremy Herrin, Alan Stacey & Rob O'Rahilly**
Associate Producer & General Manager	**Alecia Marshall**
Casting Director	**Jessica Ronane**
Creative Associate	**Lucie Lovatt**
Production Coordinator	**Grace Nelder**
Head of Technical & Production	**Sacha Milroy**

www.secondhalfproductions.co.uk

ELEANOR LLOYD
PRODUCTIONS

Current productions include the site-specific production of *Witness For The Prosecution,* which has performed in a specially created theatre in London's County Hall since 2017 and *Vardy v Rooney: The Wagatha Christie Trial.* Forthcoming productions include *The Collaboration* with Paul Bettany and Jeremy Pope which played the Young Vic in 2022 and will open at The Freidman Theater on Broadway in December 2022 and is being made into a feature film.

Recent productions include *Constellations* with 4 different casts which played in rep at the Vaudeville Theatre, winning two 2021 Olivier Awards and new play *Emilia,* which transferred from Shakespeare's Globe to the Vaudeville Theatre and won three 2020 Olivier Awards.

Other recent productions include West End transfers of *Nell Gwynn*, *My Night with Reg* and *Handbagged,* West End and Broadway seasons of *1984* by Duncan Macmillan and Rob Icke and UK tours of *Dusty,* a new musical about Dusty Springfield by Jonathan Harvey, and *Shakespeare in Love.*

Eleanor co-owns Tilted Sessions, a live podcast production company whch is currently producing *Brown Girls Do It Too* and *Something Rhymes with Purple.* www.tiltedco.com

Eleanor is the President of the Society of London Theatre (SOLT) and sits on the Boards of Stage One and Theatre503.

Producer	**Eleanor Lloyd**
General Manager and Associate Producer	**Jack Bull**
Creative Associate	**Lisa Spirling**
Production and Creative Associate	**Hart Fargo**

www.elproductions.co.uk

Wessex Grove is a theatrical production company set up by Benjamin Lowy and Emily Vaughan-Barratt in 2020.

Current and upcoming productions include: *Lemons Lemons Lemons Lemons Lemons* at the Harold Pinter Theatre; *One Woman Show* at the Ambassadors Theatre; *Best of Enemies* at the Noël Coward Theatre; *Mother Goose* at the Duke of York's Theatre and UK Tour; *Cabaret* at the Kit Kat Club, Playhouse Theatre; *The Doctor* at the Duke of York's Theatre.

Recent productions include: *Constellations* at the Vaudeville Theatre, winner of the Olivier Award for Best Revival; *Mad House* at the Ambassadors Theatre; *The Seagull* at the Harold Pinter Theatre; *Cyrano de Bergerac* at the Harold Pinter Theatre, Glasgow Theatre Royal and Brooklyn Academy of Music; and *The New Tomorrow Festival* at the Young Vic.

Producers	**Benjamin Lowy & Emily Vaughan-Barratt**
General Manager	**Tom Powis**
Production Coordinator	**Sarah Alford-Smith**
Production Coordinator	**Hugh Summers**
Administrator	**Eloise Kenny-Ryder**
Executive & Production Assistant	**Max Hoffman**

www.wessexgrove.com

Young Vic

The **Young Vic** Theatre has been one of London's leading theatres for more than 50 years. We foster emerging talent and collaborate with some of the world's finest directors, performers and creatives; creating award-winning productions which engage with the world we live in.

Built upon the principles of access, innovation, and community, the Young Vic stands out for balancing audacious commercial success and artistic flair with genuine grassroots social impact change in our neighbourhood.

Current and upcoming productions include: the world premiere of *Mandela* the musical; and in the West End, *Best of Enemies* at the Noël Coward Theatre and Rodgers & Hammerstein's *Oklahoma!* at Wyndham's Theatre; and on Broadway, *Death of a Salesman* at the Hudson Theatre and *The Collaboration* at Manhattan Theatre Club's Samuel J. Friedman Theatre.

Artistic Director   **Kwame Kwei-Armah**

Executive Director   **Lucy Davies**

www.youngvic.org

Headlong

Headlong is one of the most ambitious and exciting theatre companies in the UK, creating exhilarating contemporary theatre: a provocative mix of innovative new writing, reimagined classics and influential twentieth century plays that illuminate our world. Headlong makes bold, ground-breaking productions with some of the UK's finest artists. We take these industry-leading, award-winning shows around the country and beyond, in theatres and online, attracting new audiences of all ages and backgrounds. We make work with and for people who are marginalised by the industry and engage as deeply as we can with these communities as this helps us become better at what we do. Previous Headlong productions include *Jitney, Corrina, Corrina, After Life, People, Places and Things, The Nether, This House, Labour of Love* and *Enron*.

Artistic Director and Joint CEO   **Holly Race Roughan**

Executive Director and Joint CEO   **Lisa Maguire**

Headlong's co-commission of *Best of Enemies* is generously supported by Cockayne – Grants for the Arts, The London Community Foundation and The John Ellerman Foundation.

Supported using public funding by
**ARTS COUNCIL
ENGLAND**

www.headlong.co.uk

Best of Enemies

Cast

Gore Vidal
William F. Buckley Jr
An ensemble of actors play the following roles:
Howard K. Smith, *ABC news anchor*
James Baldwin, *writer, Gore's friend*
Patricia Buckley, *William's wife*
Matt, *Gore's researcher*
Elmer Lower, *ABC news president*
David Brinkley, *NBC anchor*
William Sheehan, *ABC news producer*
Chet Huntley, *NBC anchor*
George Merlis, *ABC marketing man*
Walter Cronkite, *CBS anchor*
Andy Warhol, *artist, friend*
Mayor Daley, *Mayor of Chicago*
Frank Meyer, *William's publisher*
Howard Austen, *Gore's partner*
Brooke Gladstone, *academic*
ABC Reporter
Cambridge President
Production Manager
Press / Interviewers / Partygoers

And the same ensemble, either through lip-syncing or literal performance, give bursts from pop culture and political figures including:

Harry Belafonte, Aretha Franklin, Tariq Ali, Enoch Powell, Martin Luther King Jr, Arthur Miller, Petula Clark, Paul Newman, Norman St John Stevas, Senator Ribicoff

Setting

The majority of the action could feel like it takes place on the soundstage of a television studio, which can transform equally into the floor of a political convention, or a university debating society, or a cabaret lounge.

Either way, it's a bear-pit where the audience are ever-present, either acting as studio audience members, or students, voters, or protestors.

Prologue

A TV soundstage in Chicago, the summer of 1968.

Something has just happened. There is heavy breathing coming over the sound system, as we find:

In two chairs, facing one another, **Gore Vidal** *and* **William F. Buckley**.

They're shaken – catching their breath – staring at one another – cameras pointing – and surrounding crew and production staff looking at them in shock.

Some audio feedback seems to grow and grow and grow and –

– snap. We're back in some form of reality. Studio lights, an 'On Air' sign.

Howard K. Smith, *the news anchor, speaking from his news desk nearby.*

Howard K. Smith   I – I think we have run out of time, and I thank you very much for the discussion. There was a little more heat, and a little less light than usual, but it was still – very worth hearing …

We'll be right back.

Then, the 'off air' studio lights snap back up.

Someone in our audience stands, slowly.

(Sometimes characters will come from, or return to, the TV studio audience where our real audience sit.)

Audience Member   Did you see that? Were you watching?

Howard *leaves his desk, approaching producer* **William Sheehan**.

Howard K. Smith   Sheehan, is he – Jesus, is he allowed to say that?

William Sheehan   I mean, we were live, and he did say it. So …

Some phones around him start to ring.

William Sheehan   Ah shit, *shit*. (*Answers one*.) Yes?!

Audience Member   Was anybody watching?

A beat. One of our first witnesses comes forward.

James Baldwin   *I* was watching. 'The Whole World was watching.'

Patricia Buckley   I was watching. From Bill's trailer. And frankly I do wish everybody would calm down –

Aretha Franklin   I'm calm. I want to tell you that I am calm. But I *was* watching.

On set, **Buckley** *and* **Vidal** *are removing their microphone sets.*

Buckley (*to an assistant*)   Please, can you get this off me? Please?

Elmer Lower, *the ABC Head of News, marches onto set towards the production staff.*

Elmer Lower   What in Jesus goddamn Christ?!

William Sheehan   Boss, we know, we know, look –

Elmer Lower   The phone calls I'm getting –

William Sheehan   Yeah ok, some, some sponsors are freaking out a bit, but –

Elmer Lower   Spons– ... forget them, my own mother just called! Furious!

Tariq Ali (*standing*)   The thing we must remember – uh, do we need to introduce ourselves first? Tariq Ali.

Howard K. Smith, *forever the professional, leaps into host mode, introducing speakers.*

Howard K. Smith   Mr Ali, please.

Tariq Ali   What we must remember is that such pivotal moments in our history do not occur in a void. Anger, discord, violence doesn't just 'erupt' from nowhere, they emerge slowly. This was a long time coming. And its consequences – linger …

Elmer Lower   My mom!

Buckley *and* **Vidal** *have finally removed their mic packs and are leaving, passing one another.*

Vidal   Well. We certainly gave them their money's worth tonight.

A moment, they split.

James Baldwin   I have always said that art is a kind of confession.

Howard K. Smith   Mr James Baldwin.

James Baldwin   I don't mean to imply that what we witnessed here was 'art', by any means. People are upset. I understand that. They want to, and believe, that they live inside a particular reality. And then the veil is lifted. And one is suddenly forced to witness not what we would prefer to be, but instead, who we really are. As a country. As people. That, I'm afraid, is who you are, here tonight. What we all are here for. We're here to 'witness'.

Tariq Ali   It's tempting to overstate the significance of such moments, of course –

Aretha Franklin   It's not an overstatement.

Howard K. Smith   Aretha Franklin –

Aretha Franklin   You don't have to announce *me*, honey, they know who I am.

And I was there. That summer, of '68.

It *was* a turning point. A shift, I saw it. In our culture. In how we literally 'talk', to one another …

Patricia Buckley   Bill?

Buckley *has arrived in the dressing room, his wife is here. A beat, as he tries to compose himself.*

Buckley   That was a disaster. Did that really happen? Is this real, am I dreaming?

Elmer Lower (*barging in*)   Bill, what on earth –?!

Buckley   Did people hear that? Elmer –

Elmer Lower   We're editing it out, when it airs on the West Coast, look, this is my station and when I say –

Buckley   Could people *hear* it, over the, the crosstalk? There was a lot of – of shouting –

Elmer Lower   People … people heard it. (*As* **Sheehan** *arrives.*) Where the hell is Vidal?

William Sheehan   I think he's already talking to the press.

Elmer Lower   Of course he is!

The producers leave.

Patricia Buckley   Bill … ?

Buckley *paces, heads in his hands.*

James Baldwin   Some of us, I suppose, are spared such trauma. The trauma of discovering that the world is not so full of kindness, and consensus. Yes, some of us have known that for a very long time. But I understand why *you* are shocked to witness it. Here now, in full colour, for all to see.

Aretha Franklin   It was a foreshadowing, it was. Of an unhappy future.

(*At the audience.*) The one you're all living in today.

Buckley *turns to* **Patricia**.

Buckley   How in God's name did this happen?

Act One

Scene One – 'New York'

From the darkness, a 1960s television screen slowly flickers on.

It warms up slowly, its blue light static growing brighter, and brighter, coming to life …

Ping. The 'NBC' *logo.*

Chet Huntley *and* **David Brinkley** *spin in their chairs with an all-white American smile.*

(Their accents are from a bygone age – crisp, clipped, authoritative, reassuring …)

Chet Huntley   This is NBC News. I'm Chet Huntley.

David Brinkley   And I'm David Brinkley. This is the Huntley-Brinkley report assembled for television, every weekday night, by the world's largest broadcast news organisation – NBC.

Ping. Next up, the 'CBS' *logo.*

Walter Cronkite, *the paternalistic 'Uncle Walter' of news anchors, leaning seriously on his desk.*

Walter Cronkite   Direct from our newsroom in New York, this is CBS Evening News, with Walter Cronkite. Good evening.

Ping. Finally the 'ABC' logo. But no one is lit, just an empty spot.

Behold, the lessprofessional, lessfunded, fledgling network.

Howard K. Smith   Shouldn't I be in the frame?

Producer's Voice   My apologies, one second.

Howard K. Smith   Take your time.

Producer's Voice   Twelve seconds to air.

Howard K. Smith   Not too much time.

The lights find him.

Howard K. Smith   Oh good, look at that, I exist. You can hold that call with my therapist.

Producer's Voice   Seven seconds.

Howard K. Smith   May I ask, was there any news today and if so may I see it, please?

A hand slides some paper over to him.

Thank you. What do we have, war, pestilence, plague, the whole ball of wax, marvellous. Well I suppose as we're here, we may as tell people.

Lights, 'on air'.

This is ABC News, welcome, I'm Howard K. Smith.

All men light their pipes and step into the same space for –

A magazine shoot. TV Guide *front cover – 'The Network Anchor Men'.*

TV Guide Interviewer   Gentlemen, welcome. And thank you for agreeing to come together for this interview.

Chet Huntley   Pleasure. Walter.

Cronkite   Chet. David.

David Brinkley   Walter, good to see you. Ah, Howard. How are you?

Howard K. Smith   Doing just fine, thank you David. Just fine.

Photographer   Gentlemen, if you please?

They pose.

Flash, flash.

We may see the image, somewhere, maybe.

TV Guide Interviewer   So ...

They sit for the interview, continually lighting their pipes.

TV Guide Interviewer   1968 is an election year. All three of your networks will be covering the Conventions, in Miami Beach for the Republicans and Chicago for the Democrats. And just as those Presidential candidates will be vying for delegates, aren't you also in a kind of competition with one another? For viewers?

Walter Cronkite   If you want to talk about 'competition', and 'strategy', you should speak to the network presidents, or the Marketing Men. Because the business side is frankly *not* our business. We are the conduits through which flows important news and –

Snap – a light hits him, flickering like a projector.

(Throughout, these interruptions will occur where our characters lip-sync to some verbatim audio from the time, hearing the unique sounds and accents of 1968, and the manner of speaking, and debate.)

Walter Cronkite   'From Dallas, Texas, newsflash, apparently official. President Kennedy died at 1pm, Central Standard time, two o' clock Eastern Standard Time, some 38 minutes ago.'

Long pause, removes his glasses, gathers himself, replaces his glasses.

'Vice Pres Lyndon Johnson has left the hospital in, uh, Dallas, but we don't know to where he has proceeded. Presumably, uh he will be taking the oath of office, shortly, and become the thirty-sixth President of the United States.'

Snap back, to where we were before.

TV Guide Interviewer   But this is a particularly important time for America. The war in Vietnam has split the country, there are signs of a, a schism, growing, between the young and the older generations; of racial divisions. Is it your job to make sense of those tensions or –

Chet Huntley   The role of the Evening News in people's homes, and of the men who steward it, is to cement opinion, not to 'disrupt'. We don't stir the pot, we cool it down.

David Brinkley   Right, we simply report, we don't express opinions. News must always come from the centre. And we invite an audience of different political stripes to calmly join us there.

Walter Cronkite   Although … yes, the centre. But that doesn't mean we don't have a responsibility, every so often, to call out something corrupt or immoral, when we are uniquely placed to see it.

(*A moment.*) I'm a Murrow Boy, what can I say? We took on Hitler, and McCarthy. But I like these young men, I do. Smooth, professional, with all their – sponsors. And such.

TV Guide Interviewer   And so your respective plans for the 1968 Conventions?

Chet Huntley   At NBC we'll be doing what we always do. Pointing the camera at the stage and broadcasting live from the first gavel to the last.

Walter Cronkite   And at CBS, we'll be broadcasting in full colour, for the first time.

David Brinkley   Oh, yes, so will we at NBC.

TV Guide Interviewer   Golly. Democracy, in full colour. Mr Smith, is that the case also for ABC? With your – if you don't mind my saying, significantly smaller audience share?

Howard K. Smith   No. I don't mind you saying that. I mind that it's true. But I don't mind you saying it.

A moment. Another photo taken – snap.

They're departing. Handshakes – byes – pats on the arm.

Walter Cronkite   Wishing you all the best, gentlemen.

David Huntley   From you, 'Uncle Walter', that means an awful lot.

Walter Cronkite (*to* **Howard** *privately*)   Howard. Remember. You can always come back.

Howard K. Smith   To be a small fish in your big pond, Walter?

(*Then.*) That's – very kind, I … I'm good.

Walter Cronkite   You hang in there.

The others leave.

Howard K. Smith   'Hang in there'?!

ABC boardroom.

Elmer *is here, with* **Sheehan** *and young marketing exec* **George Merlis**.

Howard *is pouring himself coffee, slamming about.*

Howard K. Smith   It's so damn humiliating. Sheehan, you promised me if I came here, you promised me investment, a marketing push, that the ratings would change.

William Sheehan   Well, to be fair, they have changed just – in the other direction. But –

Howard K. Smith   'ABC.' You know what they call us, behind our back? The '*Almost* Broadcasting Company'.

George Merlis (*chuckling*)   'Almost', that's –

Howard K. Smith   It's not funny! Who is this?

William Sheehan   George Merlis, from marketing.

Howard K. Smith   This is a guy from marketing and he's *laughing* at how much we're tanking. Third, out of three! If there were four networks, we'd be fifth. I overheard a guy in Mortimer's the other night joking that the way to end the Vietnam War would be to broadcast it on our channel – it would be cancelled within the week!

Elmer Lower   Ok, alright –

Howard K. Smith   We've gotta turn this ship around, Elmer, I'm serious.

Elmer Lower   Here's the situation. Big year ahead for news. Haggerty understands that. But ... the budget he's allocating our department is three million dollars.

Howard K. Smith   Three million? Well that sounds like a lot. Is it? How much do Huntley and Brinkley get?

William Sheehan   ... thirty-three.

Howard K. Smith   God DAMMIT!

William Sheehan   Our ad revenues are down, the main entertainment shows aren't doing as well as –

Howard K. Smith   What about that, that crass pile of nonsense they screen at eight, the, the, the one with the nun.

George Merlis   The Flying Nun?

Howard K. Smith   I've never seen it but –

William Sheehan   It's exactly what it sounds like, it's a nun who, who flies, around Puerto Rico, you know ... solving crimes, I ...

Howard K. Smith   I thought the purpose of such dross was to draw in viewers and therefore advertisers. Otherwise what the hell is it for? Are we not now going full colour, then, because –?

Elmer Lower   No, we are. Haggerty is insisting on that.

George Merlis   You know, the show doesn't say she can actually 'fly'; the nun.

(*Off their looks.*) It's just the winds, coming in off the Atlantic, that catch her – her habit.

It's about uplift –

Elmer Lower   Look we're just going to have to innovate. Come up with an exciting, new way to cover the Conventions that doesn't cost the earth.

(*Clapping his hands.*) Up on your feet, all o' yer, we're going to generate ideas.

Howard K. Smith   Feet? I'm a news anchor, Elmer, I think best on my ass.

Elmer Lower   Come on, it's called a 'stand-up meeting', gets the blood flowing, frees your mind. Merlis, Sheehan, up. Shake it out.

They all do, hopping up and down, shaking their hands.

Elmer Lower   It's a Californian invention, all the rage on the West Coast.

Tariq Ali   Actually ...

He rises from his position, to the audience.

... 'stand-up meetings' were a tradition of the English Privy Council, dating back to ooh, 1708? Sorry, to be that person it's just, you know ... the Californians didn't invent everything.

(*Gesturing they carry on.*) Please.

A time jump – jackets are now off, cigarettes have been lit, some ideas written on a board.

William Sheehan   ABC's 'Unconventional Convention Coverage'.

George Merlis   I really like it. It's fun.

Elmer Lower   Yeah, and it makes it look like it's a *choice* to, you know –

Howard K. Smith   – be terrible.

Elmer Lower   Right.

William Sheehan   Right; instead of rolling coverage throughout the day, we do one evening round-up show. Hosted by Howard, with his broadcasting experience.

But uh … (*clears his throat*) one new thought was that it, it might be interesting to invite real people onto the show.

Howard K. Smith   'Real people'? You mean like 'voters'?

William Sheehan   Oh, no I meant like celebrities.

Howard K. Smith   Oh thank God.

George Merlis   Smart people. From the world of film, literature.

Howard K. Smith   Non-reporters? To offer up what, exactly?

William Sheehan   Well. 'Opinions.'

Howard K. Smith   … O-pin-ions? The news deals in facts? Elmer?!

Elmer Lower   Look. I know you think I'm just the cynical executive now, but I was there with you in Berlin. Remember? Rebuilding the press, for the once-oppressed people. I'll bet I know and care more about the true value of news than any chuckleheads over the road. But for it to have value, you gotta be *heard*. We need people that'll draw audiences to us.

Howard K. Smith   … Who?

William F. Buckley Jr *delivering a measured, calm address to camera, for an interview.*

Buckley   We have to ask ourselves, why are the races unreconciled? Why does poverty persevere? Why are the young disenchanted? Why do the birds sing so unhappily? It is easy be carried away. And yet there is something in the system that warns us, warns that America had better strike out on a different course rather than face asphyxiation by liberal premises. I'm William F. Buckley in New York.

Beat. Then with his trademark grin –

Buckley   Perfect. (*Laughs*) How 'bout that, first take.

Wasn't that perfect, my love, aren't you glad you married someone so handsome and talented?

The caustic **Patricia Buckley**, *glamorous, forever smoking.*

Patricia Buckley   Actually I thought I'd married a writer and a scholar. 'Tel-e-vision', goodness me, what on earth am I going to tell our friends?

Buckley   You tell them, my little buttercup, that your husband is an exciting new breed of High Society. A 'public intellectual'.

Patricia Buckley   A true intellectual would have the grace to stay private about it, not show off to the world.

Buckley   A 'show off'. (*Laughing.*) Ye-es.

Production Manager   Onto the next set-up.
And – action.

Buckley (*serious again, dashing for the camera*)   It is our duty, to ask these very serious questions, in a very serious manner, in order to protect our American experiment from the encroaching immorality of the new promiscuous society, and to stay true to the Christian values our Founders built this nation upon …

We then find:

Gore Vidal, *being interviewed for the cover of* Time Magazine *for his new book.*

Vidal   My new book is about a man who becomes a woman, who becomes a man again, who, *when* she's a woman, she sodomises a man using a strap-on dildo–

Time Interviewer   I – I'm not sure we can say that?

Vidal   Which, sodomy or dildo? Really, in *Time Magazine*?

Time Interviewer   Why have you chosen to write *Myra*, Mr Vidal? A transexual. Is America really ready?

Vidal   I don't care if America is 'ready', I am ready. And because it occurred to me that the central drive in human beings is power. And that has always been my theme.

And it occurred to me about sexual relations, how indeed much of it is not based upon any pleasure principle or even a procreative one but of people Gaining Power over others. And given that it is as natural to be homosexual as it is to be heterosexual, the difference between the two is about the difference between someone who has brown eyes and blue eyes –

Time Interviewer   I, well I mean … who says so?

Vidal   I say so. It has been a completely natural act since the beginning of time. Some may have your own narrow views of what is correct sexual behaviour. I happen to disagree with it, and I think many people do. (*Smiles, mischievously.*)

Gore Vidal's *New York apartment.*

A New Year's Eve party. Cocktails and canapes circle on trays for the trendiest crowd in town. He holds court.

All   Cheers!

Party Guest   Is it true, Gore, Hollywood wants Myra?

Vidal   Oh now Patty, you know I don't trade in rumour or gossip.

Laughter.

We call Hollywood an 'industry', well an industry manufactures things for consumption. And the only thing Hollywood can be said to manufacture is comforting lies that pacify us into accepting the American Dream, or rather the American Myth, inoculating us to believe that the West is in the ascendance when it is in fact in collapse. So why on earth would I send dear sweet Myra all the way to Hollywood?

Having said that, yes, I've sold them the rights and it's happening.

Party Guest   Gore!

Vidal   A man's gotta eat! (*Seeing* **Matt**, *who has shyly come over*.) And speaking of – hello. And you are?

Matt   Oh I uh – Matt, I came, with a friend –

Vidal   Did you now. Well welcome Matt, to our little gathering of castaways and degenerates.

Party Guest   This from the man on the front cover of *Time Magazine!*

Vidal   Myra is the front cover, she operates entirely independently from me. I watch with horrified fascination like the rest of you. Not that anybody's buying books any more. Right, James? Are people buying our books?

James Baldwin (*coming over*)   Our books, or any books?

Vidal   Oh I don't care about other people's books, James. Ours!

James Baldwin   I should like to think so. Books for me, though I read them entirely alone, made me realise that I wasn't. They were my window into the world.

Vidal   Yes well that window, I'm afraid, is now television. Quite literally; d'you know, there are people who now arrange their furniture around them. (*At laughter.*) I'm serious. Where once an armchair might face a view, or a nice painting –

Party Guest   One of your pieces, Andy!

Andy Warhol   Oh. I just want everyone to be happy, really. Just …

They wait, but nothing else comes. **Vidal** *rolling his eyes and pushing on.*

Vidal   Yes, well, television has its downsides. You know when I ran for Congress in 1960, I gave dozens of appearances for that demonic, infantilizing little lens, and my opponent for the seat gave absolutely none. And who do you think won?!

Laughter.

Party Guest   And what are your hopes and dreams for 1968? For the party to continue? Bobby Kennedy in the White House?

Vidal   What's my golden rule?! Do not mention that name in this house!

Party Guest   Why *did* you fall out? Different beliefs?

Vidal   Yeah sort of, in that I have some, and he doesn't. No, I fear what awaits us this year is not peace and parties. Largely because where there was consensus, there is growing divergence. Where once there was hope, now there is anger. And so bluntly speaking – I think there'll be war.

Matt   Aren't we already at war?

Vidal   Not war abroad, war here, in America. And perhaps there should be, you know, *perhaps* there *should* be. And it'll get ugly and you're going to have to pick a side.

Party Guest   Mr Baldwin, what do you think? Is Gore just playing the playwright, yes? Over dramatic!

James Baldwin   Well –

Snap –

The Cambridge Union –

James Baldwin   'I am stating very seriously, and this is not an overstatement. That *I* picked the cotton. And *I* carried it to market. And *I* built the railroads, under someone else's whip, for nothing. For nothing.'

Snap back –

James Baldwin   ... I don't know. Andy?

Andy Warhol   I can't bear ugliness. It's so ... the opposite of ... you know.

He wanders again, everyone waits, and **Vidal** *sighs. To a* **Waiter**.

Vidal   More drinks please, let's lubricate our passage out of this year and into the dark cavernous hole of the next.

Waiter   A phone call for you, Mr Vidal.

He steps away. Briefly with the **Party Guest**.

Party Guest   Don't leave us with Andy for too long, I've never met a buzz he couldn't kill.

Vidal   Ah yes. The first man I ever met with an IQ lower than 60 and yet somehow a genius. Just think of him as an attractive centrepiece I bought along as decoration. One moment.

In a separate space, he takes up a receiver.

Vidal   Hello?

James Baldwin *arrives here too, smoking, listening privately.*

Vidal   Why? What did they say?

Oh come on, there must be a – ...

Eric, I need this, I need to stay – visible, it's –

Oh I can tone down all that. The whole East-coast intellectual ... I can be 'perky'. 'Winning.'

Look just get me on it.

Phone down. Without turning ...

Go on.

James Baldwin   I'm saying nothing.

Vidal   Hah.

James Baldwin   Only that you shouldn't feel you have to exaggerate out there your opposition to that which you are secretly drawn to. No one would judge you.

Vidal   Judge me what, James? 'Fame.' I'm not drawn to it, it's just that's the new currency and so what am I meant to do?

James Baldwin   I almost believe you.

Vidal (*paces, then*)   It's hard to make a living telling Americans something they don't want to hear.

James Baldwin   You really don't have to explain that to me.

And which show is this (*at the phone*), that you're trying to get on?

Vidal   Oh some game show on CBS. I don't know. All I know from now on, a man should never turn down two things. Sex, and appearing on television.

James Baldwin   It's Bobby, isn't it? (*No response.*) I get it. You thought it would be *you*. After Jack. It's alright, Gore, a lot of us did.

Vidal   … Flamboyant playwrights don't lead nations.

James Baldwin   Well what can they lead? The 'conversation'? Perhaps?

Vidal (*beat, looking back at the phone*)   … Perhaps.

James Baldwin   Nice party, Gore. No Tennessee, no Truman tonight?

Vidal   Oh, knowing Tennessee, he's probably off somewhere, falling in love.

And knowing Truman, no doubt the opposite.

Are you alright?

James Baldwin *swigs the drink in his glass, considering this. As he's leaving …*

James Baldwin   Try to stay happy, Gore. Be good, and be happy.

Meanwhile, in **Buckley**'s *apartment across town …*

The end of a civilised dinner from **Buckley** *and* **Patricia**, *with* **Frank Meyer**, *his publisher.*

Buckley   Now isn't this a more pleasant way to see in the new year than any of those ghastly parties we were invited too. Conversation around the dinner table.

Frank Meyer (*holding it up*)   And a celebration of another year of our 'National Review'! Standing alone but proud, introducing Conservative ideas to America. A-thank you.

Patricia Buckley   Bill come on, champagne for the toast; tradition, you like traditions.

Buckley   Yes but, I loathe champagne. See how much quiet dignity my whisky has just sitting there. And then look at champagne. The attention seeker of drinks.

Frank Meyer   Well. Speaking of attention seeking –

Buckley   Oh now Frank, enough, you've made your point –

Frank Meyer   I'm just saying. This is more than a magazine, it's a Movement, and we don't want to jeopardise that by cheapening it on television.

Buckley   It's just a meeting with the producers, and you see the problem, Frank, is there's nothing cheap about running a political magazine for a currently very niche readership.

Patricia Buckley   You're telling me. It's exhausting, fundraising as a Conservative in New York. The problem is I'm too damn good at it.

Buckley   Yes, well that's because the Liberal Orthodoxy has infected every corner of the political and media class. What have we had now? Four of the last five presidents,

Democrat. A dominance of left-wing ideas for over 30 years, and they'll likely dominate for 30 more if the swivel-eyed cranks in the Republican Party can't be marginalised.

Frank Meyer   Hey, some of those swivel-eyed cranks are our subscribers.

Patricia Buckley   Yes, and a lot of them are racist. (*Then:*) What, I've met them, I'm right.

Buckley   She is right. What we need is a respectable, dignified Conservatism, as – if you'll allow me the presumption – represented by yours truly.

Frank Meyer   And you can be respectable and dignified on Network Television?

Buckley   You just watch me.

He sits himself at his harpsichord, and begins to play. Gentle, and soothing.

All   Five, four, three, two, one, Happy New Year!

We'll take a cup of kindness yet

For the days of Auld Lang …

At **Vidal***'s party – music and dancing.*

Fireworks and banners, we ring in – '1968'.

Vidal *finds a young man to kiss –* **Matt***, a college student – whom he leads away. As he goes –*

The two men somehow seem to clock each other.

The 'ABC' boardroom.

Buckley *being pitched to by the executives.*

Buckley   So let me see if I have this right …

William Sheehan   We simply pit a well-known Republican supporter against a well-known Democrat and listen to them exchange views live on television during the week of each national convention.

Elmer Lower   It's only what you do already, William, on your own TV programme, the, the – (*clicking at* **George**). George –

George Merlis   *Firing Line.*

Elmer Lower   – *Firing Line.* People with different opinions, politely talking it out.

William Sheehan   Our sincere desire is to elevate the public discourse. Not cheapen it.

Buckley   And what's the real reason?

William Sheehan   That's the reason.

Buckley   Well. Of course really, although you're saying a 'Republican' versus a 'Democrat', the questions facing our society now go way beyond party lines. These are philosophical questions we're wrestling with. And indeed I should need to be free to criticise the Republican plank as much as the Democratic one, especially if the Republicans once again nominate a candidate from the Old Right.

So what you're really saying – may I?

George Merlis (*handing him a pen*)   Sure.

Buckley *rewrites on the flip chart.*

Buckley   … is that you want a 'Conservative', versus a 'Liberal'.

(*Tapping it.*) This will be the new dividing line of America and should be represented thus.

Elmer Lower   See? I already feel smarter. Don't you both? Already feel –?

Buckley (*sitting again*)   And who precisely will be my adversary?

Elmer Lower   We wanted to come to you first. We'll build this thing around you. Who would you like? Who would you *not* like? Haha.

Buckley   Well. I would refuse to appear on air with an actual communist.

George Merlis (*writing*)   Communist, ahuh.

Buckley   And then the only other person I wouldn't appear with would be Gore Vidal.

A moment.

William Sheehan   Oh ok. Why's that?

Buckley   Lots of reasons, really. We disagreed on David Susskind's talk show, a couple years back. I think his politics are frankly pretty extreme. He's a performer, more than he is a serious dissector of our political landscape.

But I suppose the main reason is – I don't trust him.

William Sheehan   Oh.

Buckley   Yah.

William Sheehan   Trust him, with regards –?

Buckley   To play by the rules.

Elmer Lower   Well. That's good to know. You speak of 'trust', William. Just to reassure you. In recent years, in every poll, the institution which most Americans now place the most 'trust' – is television.

And. We don't see this little experiment changing that. And it *is* an experiment, a shot in the dark, it might work, might not, we'll learn things along the way.

Buckley (*seeing the writing on the board*)   'Unconventional Convention Coverage.'

Elmer Lower   That's right! Only on ABC! Haha.

Buckley   … Yah. Well, count me in.

Elmer/William/George   Great!

Snap, lights hit –

ABC Newsroom. **Vidal** *is here now, with* **Elmer**, **William** *and* **George**.

Vidal   Well. I have to say that I'm not entirely un-interested by the prospect. If the format is right, which I should like some input into. You're not expecting … how can I put this … me to 'dumb it down', for your audience –

Elmer Lower   Well, we want them to be able to Follow Along, Gore, but you can bring all your references, sure. You know, Pericles, Shakespeare. All that shit.

Vidal   All that shit, got it.

And Mr Buckley? Do you think he'll be on board and ABC viewers will be able to handle his peculiar tics? (*Mimics one.*)

Elmer Lower   Sure. I mean, he's got the way he talks, and you've got the way you talk.

Vidal   We haven't exactly revelled in each other's company on prior occasions.

William Sheehan   Oh, really? He didn't say.

Vidal   Yes, I may have once referred to the Buckley Family as being the sort of 'Sick Kennedys'. Which for some reason I think he took personally. Though of course, the political *is* now the personal. It's how we identify, and who we identify with. That sort of goes to the very heart of the New Left.

Elmer Lower   The New Left? Where does that come from, the –

Vidal   It's led by a younger generation, an exciting generation, and concerns itself less with the old Marxist preoccupations of social *class*, and more of – social *justice*. Gay rights, abortion, black rights, women's rights.

George   And, Mr Vidal, you wouldn't mind –

Vidal   And you are?

George Merlis   Uh George. Marketing. You wouldn't mind doing some press?

Vidal   Hello George Marketing. And no, I don't mind.

George Merlis   Great. We'd love to get people talking, about this.

Vidal   You want to get Buckley and I talking. And then you want people talking about that.

Elmer Lower   And then, who knows. Maybe those people will start talking to Each Other. After all. Isn't that what America needs, right now?

Vidal   Let's find out, shall we?

All   Great!

ABC newsroom.

Howard K. Smith   Quite incredible scenes in Paris, as tens of thousands of students began rioting in the streets, and occupying major universities as part of a General Strike that could bring the Republic to its knees.

CBS newsroom.

Walter Cronkite   In scenes not seen before, now televised, thousands of anti-Vietnam protestors marched on the United States Embassy in London's Grosvenor Square.

Snap to –

Tariq Ali (*with loudspeaker*)   We express our solidarity with our Vietnamese friends, suffering under the oppression of the West, for committing the cardinal sin of wanting to live under a different political idea!

Then, the painfully civilised theme tune of **Buckley**'s Firing Line *TV show. As we find:*

Buckley   Welcome … to the *Firing Line*. Here we aspire to carry forward the torch of the Enlightenment, whose flame in the modern world may, yes, be fading, but still flickering, just. Where we conduct civil discussion in the old-fashioned belief that tolerance towards conflicting points of view are our only hope of arriving at a more successful society.

(*Introducing*.) Mr Enoch Powell … was kicked out of the British shadow cabinet in punishment for a speech in which he advocated an end to coloured immigration into England.

Mr Powell, your essential position seems to be –

Snap –

The projector light hits **Powell** *as he lip-syncs his 1968 'Rivers of Blood' speech.*

Enoch Powell   In this country in fifteen or twenty years, the black man will have the whip hand, over the white man.

Like the Roman, I seem to see 'the River Tiber foaming with much blood' …

Snap back –

Buckley   – that separation of culturally dissimilar people is not only sometimes necessary but even desirable –

Enoch Powell   I *would* say there is a *limit* to the number of – and I'm going to use this word in an entirely neutral sense – 'aliens' … who can be brought into a nation, without breaking the bonds of that society and setting up intolerable frictions and stresses, as damaging to one side as the other.

Buckley   But doesn't one suppose that as this population increases, you're simply dealing with *Englishmen* with a brown skin? Rather than with *Pakistanis*?

Enoch Powell   … uh, well, actually, as the numbers increase, the tendency is for separation to increase. You do in fact get a pulling apart.

Buckley   Well, I'll be pushing you to consider that point further when we return.

Buckley *steps off to take his phone call.*

Patricia   Ducky? It's Elmer Lower at ABC.

Buckley   Elmer? Yeah listen, if you wanted my participation in your mad scheme, you shouldn't have invited the one man I insisted I couldn't appear opposite.

Elmer Lower   William, we scoured, and we searched, but – he tests great, he's a genuine – you know, 'character', he's got the way he talks, and you've got the way you talk.

Buckley   Look where we are, Elmer. The political and social discord that is growing, and spreading across the globe? Do you think the framing of this new and serious mood is best served by someone as unserious as Vidal? Don't you watch my show? I can't conduct such productive, calm and good-faith exchanges with someone like him, he, he's –

Elmer Lower   I hear your concerns, William, and in recognition of your great display of magnanimity, we'd be willing to increase your fee, to ten thousand dollars.

Buckley   … Mm.

Elmer Lower   Or, we could find someone else from the Right to put in the limelight.

Buckley   … Very well.

Scene Two – 'Miami'

The 'Elephant' symbol of the Republican Party lights up with a ting somewhere.

Behold, all the Americana, banners and balloons of a Republican National Convention.

Gore Vidal *and* **William F. Buckley** *arrive at the Convention.*

Suddenly, snap –

Andy Warhol, *hands covered in red paint perhaps, who joins in with the dance. He is shot.*

It morphs into something slower, weirder, darker, as we find **Martin Luther King Jr**.

Martin Luther King Jr   Something is happening in our world. The masses of people are rising up. And wherever they are assembled today, whether they are in Johannesburg, South Africa; Nairobi, Kenya; Accra, Ghana; New York City; Atlanta, Georgia; Jackson, Mississippi; or Memphis, Tennessee – the cry is always the same: 'We want to be free.'

Vidal *is watching.*

King *disappears.*

Aretha *stands from the audience, and then leaves …*

A press pack is gathered around **Elmer Lower** *at the Convention.*

Elmer Lower   What is happening this year, what is happening in America, the assassination of Reverend King … it's utterly senseless. But it is beholden on us to try and make sense of it. That's one of the motivating factors behind our 'Unconventional Convention Coverage' this year. To talk, to one another.

Snap to –

Bobby Kennedy   What I think is quite clear … is that we *can* work together, in the last analysis. And that what has been going on within the United States over the period of the last three years, the divisions, the violence, the disenchantment with our society, the divisions whether it's between blacks and whites, between the poor and more affluent, or between age groups or on the war in Vietnam, is that we can start to work together, we are a great country, and a selfish country, and a compassionate country. And I intend to make that my basis for running over the period of the next few months …

Howard K. Smith   Senator Robert Kennedy there, claiming victory in the California Democratic primary. The next major event on the political scene – the Republican National Convention, in Miami. We'll be there. This is Howard K. Smith.

Snap, into the real –

Ladies and Gentlemen, we've kept the air on because we've heard an alarming report that Robert Kennedy was shot leaving that ballroom at the Ambassador Hotel. A very loud noise like a clap of thunder. We await more. Robert Kennedy of course, who lost his brother to an assassin's bullet …

(*Getting more news.*) One of our assistant directors was one of those who was shot. An ABC assistant director, working on this programme … shot in the hand.

In **Vidal**'s *suite.* **Matt** *here, watching.*

Matt   Are you alright?

It's ok to feel complicated and contradictory things about things that are complicated and contradictory.

Vidal   Thank you for that permission.

Matt   What went so wrong, between you?

Vidal   … oh, many things. We were both in love with his brother, of course, but in different ways. And Jackie and I, we shared a step-father, we were very close. Which I think threatened Robert. His place, in the circle …

Matt   Must have been quite something. To be a part of that. Camelot. Even for a time.

Vidal   … (*Snapping out of it.*) We are where we are. And it's where I foretold we would be. The tree of liberty, it appears, must occasionally be watered with blood.

What is happening? Andy shot. Martin and Bobby gone …

The world feels on fire. I hadn't expected this – backdrop. When I agreed to take to the stage …

Matt   Well. Maybe some things need burning down. Can't you feel it? People my age, out on the streets, fighting for more radical change?

You could become an entire generation's pin up, Gore, with these appearances.

Vidal   *Debates* And pin-up? Hah. (*A moment, then:*) Well anyway, I'm glad you came to Miami, Matthew. I could do with your help.

Matt   You're asking for my help? Gore! I'd love to. You mean, work up some arguments and ideas? Role play some, some (*fencing*), verbal thrusts and parries and blocks?

Vidal   Excuse me, post-graduate, I already have the arguments and ideas, they form the core of my very being. I meant research. I know that Buckley won't prepare, he thinks himself too much of a genius for that. Well I want to expose him, and his movement, for the bigoted, small-minded, dangerous nonsense that it is. I need quotes! Gaffes! Things he's said in the past, that have proven wrong, so I can humiliate him in the present.

With a copy of National Review.

Only I refuse to read his insult of a magazine, so if you wouldn't mind, perhaps you could. You'll need copies going back at least eight years, my publisher can help.

Matt   So I'm a dogsbody?

Vidal   But what a body. (*Kisses him.*) And I despise labels; too reductive. (*Taking hold of him suggestively.*) I like things that grow under scrutiny, not shrink ...

Back to work! What are we to expect from the other side?

In **Buckley***'s suite (we bounce back between them).*

Patricia Buckley   My-my. Could we be any higher; look at this view of the sea. ABC are investing more in this than I imagined. Better not screw it up, Bill.

Buckley   You do know this isn't my first rodeo, Ducky? And I've dispatched far tougher foes than this.

Frank Meyer   But this is *television* Bill. I'll bet it doesn't have the order of, say, your debate with Baldwin in Cambridge.

Buckley   Ahh ... yes, Cambridge. Exactly. I must channel Cambridge. The oldest debating society in the world, the greatest minds, locking intellectual horns –

Frank Meyer   He's going to try and trap you. Vidal is perhaps America's greatest talker. Thankfully you're one of America's greatest thinkers.

Patricia Buckley   I'll confess, he does make *me* laugh. Don't get me wrong, I think he's the Devil, but doesn't the Devil often have the best tunes?

Buckley   I'm not worried about Vidal. He'll have *over*-prepared. Whereas we've just been sailing for a week, resting on the open water. In a debate, the best approach is to trust you have the right instincts to be able to react in the moment.

Vidal   Buckley won't have any facts at his fingertips at all, only prejudices, which he'll work through in order – his sexism, racism, leftism, homophobia. While I shall be able to summon statements and facts from my clipboard – where is my clipboard?!

Matt   Your sword, sire! (*Handing it over.*)

Vidal   Giving time and place and statements and statistics.

Matt   Not to mention your painstakingly crafted 'ad-libs'.

Vidal   Yes, yes we need more of those. Waspish spontaneity rehearsed in advance.

Buckley   I'm not worried about Vidal's philosophy – it's hollow and wrong. I'm more worried about his … (*sighs*). His 'sense of humour'. He's going to 'quip'.

Frank Meyer   Quip?

Vidal (*brainstorming*)   He's 'almost always on the Right, and always in the wrong'?

Matt   Yes! Nice.

Buckley   He thinks he's the American Oscar Wilde.

Frank Meyer   Both fags.

Patricia Buckley   Now wait there, I happen to adore the gays –

Buckley   Oh only because they adore you. She has a whole list of them.

Patricia Buckley   It's true, I do. Fabulously sophisticated bachelors who attend opening nights with me while my hard-working husband is away.

Frank Meyer   Is he – … I mean has he ever actually said that he's –?

Vidal   I must get under his skin, make him uncomfortable. He sweats, he's a sweater, which looks dishonest on screen. Remember Nixon, the *last* time he ran? Jack Kennedy beat him because Dickie Nixon perspired under the lights, and the public no longer trusted him.

Frank Meyer   Fundamentally, if you were to lay it all out, for a popular television audience ... what do the Left believe, and how do we differ?

Perhaps a flip board, writing two columns – 'us' and 'them'. Underneath which are various topic headings.

Patricia Buckley   Well you're the former communist, Frank.

Frank Meyer   And thank God I saw the light!

Buckley   We believe in increasing the freedoms and powers of the *individual*, they fantasise in further expanding the role and responsibilities of the State.

Frank Meyer   They wouldn't if they lived in East Berlin, or Moscow, believe me!

Vidal   Naturally he believes that if big businesses and private enterprises get richer, they can perform the social functions of the state. But instead they will of course put profit before people, and our social divides and inequalities will get infinitely worse.

Buckley   That means we are for 'lower taxes' – surely a popular position – while they for 'high'.

Frank Meyer   Exactly, *they* want to take 'your money' from 'your pocket', because they think they know how to spend it better than 'you' –

Patricia Buckley   They dislike America, but we, like most Americans, are grateful to have been born here.

Matt He'll do that classic Conservative thing of equating any criticism of this country as being in some way unpatriotic. It's always a slam dunk for the Right.

Vidal Ugh, he's going to bring up my apartment in Rome, isn't he?

Matt Of course. He needs the audience to disregard you as the out-of-touch, liberal elite.

Vidal Yeah well, *he* is for sending innocent American boys to be slaughtered in Vietnam.

Frank Meyer Vietnam *is* unpopular.

Buckley I don't care. We just have to paint his pacifism as 'weak', and our patriotism as noble and strong.

Patricia Buckley As long as you remain calm, Ducky.

Buckley (*smiles*) Have you met me, Ducky?

Vidal Will he attack Myra, do you think?

Matt Maybe best to sidestep Myra.

Vidal Why, her very existence will have utterly scandalised him!

Matt You need to stop thinking of him as your target, you're trying to win over the viewing public. It's about how you convert *them*. You're never going to convert William F. Buckley.

Vidal I might not convert him, but I can annoy him. (*Gasps.*) Ooh. I know!

Buckley Oh God. He's going to call me 'Bill', isn't he?

Matt Haha. Yes, do it!

Vidal/Matt Bill! Bill! Bill!

Patricia Buckley Bill, you can be annoying too. Utterly infuriating.

Buckley   Thank you, dear.

Well I shall address him as 'Mr Vidal'. In fact perhaps I shouldn't address him directly at all? In the British House of Commons, to maintain decorum and avoid ad hominem attacks, all points go through the Speaker of the House. One never speaks to one's opponent directly.

Patricia Buckley   Howard K. Smith, the anchor, he could be your equivalent.

Buckley   Yes! Good. (*Grins.*) I'm actually now quite looking forward to it.

Patricia Buckley   Yes well try not to enjoy it too much, Bill. It's not just our reputations at stake, though that too.

Buckley   Oh really? What else?

Patricia Buckley   Ducky, look what's happening out there. We have pulled up to a fork in the road; which way, this or that. It's a battle, Bill. (*Knowingly dramatic.*) For the 'soul of America'. (*Laughs.*)

Buckley   Let's keep a little perspective, shall we? This is a late-night talk show, on the lowest-ranked network. But if I can quietly shine a light on how harmful – truly *harmful* – Vidal and his radical leftism is … I'd say that was a pretty good use of our time.

The ABC sign pings. Then flickers – then tilts – then cracks – then falls.

The *producers, in a panic. One* **Assistant Producer** *is covered in dust.*

Elmer Lower   It collapsed?! Our entire studio?!

Assistant Producer   Yeah it just – it just came down! Overnight.

Elmer Lower   Any others? NBC, CBS?

Assistant Producer   Just ours.

Elmer Lower   Of course just ours! It's Day One! And everyone is laughing at us! They were laughing before but son of a bitch and Jesus Christ –

William Sheehan   We're going to throw something together, no one'll know.

Elmer Lower *paces, thinking.*

Elmer Lower   … No. No fuck it, let 'em know. Better yet, let's tell 'em! ourselves! We own our own stories on ABC!

Suddenly a camera is pointing at **Lower**, *with* **Howard K. Smith** *doing the interview.*

Howard K. Smith   Three … two … one …

Well, Mr Lower, you're the News President of ABC. You promised the world Unconventional Convention coverage, but this is ridiculous.

Elmer Lower   Well we're sure going to be unpredictable, Howard. Indeed we've no idea what's going to happen next, which – for the viewing public – I hope is exciting.

Take tonight, two of the world's foremost brains are going to battle it out. No script, completely live. William F. Buckley and Gore Vidal. And we think the fur is sure going to fly.

Assistant Producer   Got it.

Howard *steps away, in private, mops his brow.*

David Brinkley *of NBC wanders by.*

David Brinkley   Political broadcast as 'light entertainment'? Howard?

Howard K. Smith   Wishing NBC a great convention, David. (*They shake hands.*)

Two make-up chairs, next to each other.

Gore Vidal *sits in one, as a* **Make-up** *artist arrives.*

Make-up   Any touch up?

Vidal   Yes, I think some –

Buckley *arrives. A moment.*

He sits without saying hello.

Vidal   Uh, some light foundation around here, if you could, I'm feeling blotchy today. All that late-night cramming of numbers, dates, you know.

Buckley *smiles to himself.* **Patricia** *enters, with her own beauty bag.*

Patricia Buckley   Darling. (*At* **Make-up** *and* **Vidal**.) Hello.

Vidal   Good evening.

And some spray for my hair as well.

Make-up   Anything for you, Mr Buckley?

Buckley   My wife will just run a brush through my hair. Thank you.

Make-up (*as she's touching up* **Vidal**)   Is your wife here, Mr Vidal?

Vidal   No. No wife.

The separate work is done. **Patricia** *kisses* **Buckley** *on the head.*

Patricia Buckley   Good luck.

She goes. **Vidal** *is worked on.*

Silence, as this continues for a while.

William Sheehan (*entering*)   Gentlemen, William Sheehan, producer, we met before.

So, just to take you through it, we'll do a quick pre-record of one statement each, which Howard will set you up for.

That'll play in the ad break. And then it'll just be a couple of minutes wait before we go live on air.

Also, I know this goes without saying, but this is network television – so, no use of, of, well, any bad language, profanities, or curse words. Not that I expect you gentlemen would.

Any questions?

Buckley   No.

Vidal   Nope.

William Sheehan   Very well, then follow me.

They both stand and walk –

To the area of the soundstage where their seats are.

Assistant producers help them with their mic sets and earphones as they sit.

Camera shots are arranged.

Before they're finally alone together, in their seats.

Work is done in preparation by the production staff.

Vidal *glances quite frequently over to* **Buckley**. **Buckley** *avoids his gaze.*

Silence. Until it is broken by –

Vidal   I hear the entire studio fell over, or something.

Buckley   … Is that so?

Vidal   Adds to the jeopardy, I suppose.

Buckley *scribbles in his pad.*

Howard K. Smith *arrives, shaking hands.*

Howard K. Smith   Mr Buckley. Mr Vidal. Howard.

Buckley   Pleasure.

Vidal   Hello, Howard.

Howard *goes to his anchor's desk.*

William Sheehan   Alright, pre-recorded statements please! We'll start with Mr Buckley.

Howard K. Smith   All set?

Buckley   Sure.

Lights snap down to production level.

A red light. Cameras on.

Howard K. Smith   William F. Buckley Jr.

Buckley   … My own notion, having got here just a little while ago, is that what the Miami Convention already proves is that the overwhelming amount of power happens to lie in the hands of – *Conservative* Republicans.

Smith   And Gore Vidal?

Vidal *licks his lips, ready. Sitting forward, pointedly.*

Vidal   To me the principal question is, can a political party based almost entirely upon human *greed* … nominate anyone for President for whom a majority of the American people would vote?

Beat.

William Sheehan   Great, thank you everyone.

Lights snap out of production.

Buckley *looks out, shaking his head privately at what he just heard from* **Vidal** *– 'unbelievable'.*

Vidal *sees this and smiles.*

William Sheehan   Last speeches wrapping up in the convention hall, standby to go live.

Howard K. Smith (*into his earpiece*)   Alright. Ahuh.

Elmer Lower *arrives near* **Sheehan**, *pacing.*

Elmer Lower   Alright, here we go. Shit, shit, shit, ok. Shit.

Production Manager   Sir, please, no inflammatory language, this is the news division –

William Sheehan (*whispering*)   He's the head of the –

Elmer Lower (*hissing*)   I'm the fucking head of the fucking news division –

William Sheehan   Fifteen seconds.

Fifteen seconds of anticipation …

Deep breath everybody. And five … four …

… And … lights snap down.

Red lights on. Cameras roll.

And we're 'On Air'.

Smith   For ABC News' Convention Coverage for this presidential election, two of our nation's most decided commentators have joined us this year.

They are Gore Vidal, a former Democratic candidate for Congress, but better known as an author, of among other things a play about a political convention, and William F. Buckley Jr., a former Conservative candidate for the major of New York, but better known as a columnist, commentator, and editor of the *National Review*.

Mr Buckley, who of the potential candidates do you think is, if I may steal a title from Mr Vidal, the best man?

Buckley   Oh … I'm not prepared to say. I think that several of them are highly qualified to be a good President. I think what you really mean to ask me, but are too shy, is who do I like most.

Smith *laughs*. **Vidal** *smiles. Gentle start …*

Buckley   To which my answer is that as a Conservative I am very much fetched by the programs of Mr Reagan and also of Mr Nixon.

Smith Can Mr Vidal assess those candidates for us? What do you think of –?

Vidal Well, I would come, I think, to a very different point of view.

Waits. **Buckley** *doesn't look – he hardly ever* looks *at* **Vidal**, *when not addressing him directly, whereas* **Vidal**'s *eyes are almost always on* **Buckley**.

Vidal I think we're living in revolutionary times. In which new programs are needed.

And that you're going to need somebody who can rally the young people of the country. The Negroes. The ghetto, the poor are angry, restless.

Buckley *sighs, scribbles.* **Vidal** *refers to his extensive 'research'.*

Vidal This is a terrible time, and here you have a man – Richard Nixon – who when he was in Congress he voted *against* public housing, *against* slum clearance, *against* rent control, *against* extending the minimum wage.

So if he wins we'll have nothing in the ghetto, probably, but the rising expectation of what is now revolution.

Vidal *is done, pleased, looking at* **Buckley**.

William Sheehan Ok well, so far so good? Right?

Buckley Uh, may I comment, Mr Smith?

Elmer Lower It's uh … *interesting*? Isn't it?

Howard K. Smith Please do.

Buckley Yeah …

Elmer Lower I mean … is it?

Buckley It seems to me that the earlier focus of … (*extended*) Mr Vidaaaaal here, on human greed – you do remember? – he said that he found himself wondering whether a party that was devoted to the concept of human greed could ever hope to get a majority of the American people to vote for it.

Now the author of *Myra Breckinridge* ... is well acquainted with the imperative of human greed.

Vidal   I would like to say, Bill ...

Buckley   And – (*not expecting to be interrupted*) – erm ...

Vidal   If I may say, Bill ... before you go any further, I would like to say that if there were a contest for Mr Myra Breckinridge, you would unquestionably win it. I based her entire style polemically on you. Passionate, and irrelevant.

A moment. Crew and producers look to one another – oof.

Buckley *sits up a little.*

Buckley   That's too involuted for me to follow. One of these days perhaps you'll explain it ... .

Vidal   You follow it.

Buckley   My point is ... My ... For Mr Vidal to give us the pleasure of his infrequent company by coming back from Europe where he lives in order to disdain the American democratic process and to condemn a particular party as engaged in the pursuit of human greed requires us to understand his rather eccentric definitions.

Vidal   Well, by and large, it is a party which is based upon *business* interests. They get, through big business, they get far more subsidies than the poor do. As a matter of fact we have a situation in the United States where they believe they should have socialism for the rich and free enterprise for the poor.

Buckley   The thing about ...

Vidal   The nice thing about the Republican Party is that every four years after denigrating the poor amongst themselves, and I have many quotes here from Ronald Reagan and Richard Nixon on the subject, referring to them as freeloaders and making fun of the minority groups with lovely little remarks … then every four years you get this sort of crocodile tears for the Poor People because they need their vote.

Well, I don't think that they're going to vote for any of your candidates unless by some terrible accident the Democrats get split at Chicago.

In which case Richard Nixon might very well become the next president and I shall make my occasional trips to Europe longer.

Buckley   Yes, I think a lot of people hope you will.

Some polite – if restrained – mutual chuckling, between them.

Now it is quite true that Reagan is capable of talking about freeloaders, so am I, because there *are* freeloaders. I say the Republican Party is here to do a responsible job. To suggest that they are simple here as an instrument of the exploitation of the people is to engage in a diseased kind of analysis which increasingly Mr Vidal finds to his liking. Fortunately it is not a national concern. Perhaps the Republican Party should have a platform on how to deal with Vidal. If absolutely necessary I will write it for them.

Vidal   Hah, but –

Buckley   But meanwhile –

Vidal   But meanwhile, you have written lately of your intimacy with Reagan and with Nixon and that you've discussed the Vietnam War with them and that you are satisfied with their positions. Since you are in favour of nuclear bombing North Vietnam, I'd be very worried about your kind of odd neurosis, being a friend of anybody who might be a president.

Buckley   I would be very worried too, if you had such a *grand guignol* view, but I've never advocated the nuclear bombing of North Vietnam.

Vidal   You have, I'll give you time and place if it amuses you.

Buckley   Well, you won't.

Vidal   I will –

Buckley   I advocated the *liberation* of Cuba –

Vidal   No, no Bill, don't step away from the record. You suggested the atom bombing of the North of Vietnam in your little magazine, which I do not read but I am told about, on February 23rd 1968.

Buckley   Now, Mr Vidal, who boasts of not reading something which he is prepared to misquote in the presence of the person who edits it –

Vidal   Now, Billy Buckley, the quotation is exact –

Buckley   We know –

Vidal   – the quotation is exact.

Buckley   We know that your tendency is to be *feline*, Mr Vidal –

Vidal   Yes.

Elmer Lower   Oh wow, ok, hah, um –

Buckley   – but juuuust relax, for a moment, and think very simply on this. I have not advocated – I'm not *horrified* at the prospect of –

Vidal   Bill I just quoted whole sentences to you, when and where. Are you saying you didn't say it?

Buckley   I'm saying that I didn't say it.

Vidal   Tune in / this time tomorrow …

Buckley   Your misquotations –

Vidal   … and we will have further evidence of Bill Buckley's cold warrior / turned hot –

Buckley   That's right, and about the human greed of everybody in the world except yourself. Tomorrow we'll have what Mr Vidal thinks about the Kennedys.

Vidal   Goodnight and let me tell you –

Howard K. Smith   Excuse me, gentlemen. It's been very enjoyable hearing you articulate two points of view. Thank you very much indeed.

I think I detected some unfinished lines of thought. We'll have time to follow them through tomorrow, and tomorrow, and tomorrow.

The 'On Air' lights go out. A moment, then … excitedly …

William Sheehan   Thank you, everyone!

Vidal *looks to* **Buckley**, *who is removing his mic pack, not looking back.*

Elmer Lower *hops up on stage, laughing.*

Elmer Lower   Well! Haha. That started to catch fire, I'd say, wouldn't you both?! You know I think this is going to work! You?

Vidal   Yes, I thought that most enjoyable.

Buckley *is leaving the stage.*

Elmer Lower   Until tomorrow, Bill!

Buckley   Yah.

A New York Daily News **Reporter** *dictating a review.*

Reporter   Well, exclamation point. Move over Nixon and Reagan, exclamation point. The beauty of Buckley and Vidal disliking one another intensely and both gifted in invective, dash, they are far and away the best infighters in Miami Beach, exclamation point, end quote.

Vidal *and* **Elmer Lower** *holding court with a press gaggle.*

Vidal   I would say that, as I suspected, Billy Buckley doesn't like to hear his own words, and his own viewpoints, repeated back to him, and frankly I don't blame him at all.

Press Gaggle   Mr Lower, you're parading Mr Vidal around the Convention Hall bars like your prize fighter – are we calling debate one for Gore?

Elmer Lower   That's for the viewing public to decide – and I've just heard that viewing public is up 250,000 American homes on our coverage last year. So I suggest our friendly rivals watch out too because ABC's a'coming!

*Vidal kisses **Matt** when he locates him, an affectionate, victorious hug.*

The next day –

Buckley *with the producers.*

Buckley   What I'm suggesting is a slight refinement of the format, that's all. No crosstalk, none of this interjecting. Smith asks a question, I get two minutes to respond, and then Vidal does the same. Like a real debating society – like Cambridge. Did you not see my famous debate with his friend James Baldwin at Cambridge University, three years ago.

*Flash – a spotlight on **George** as he becomes **James**.*

Buckley *watching.*

James Baldwin   It comes as a great shock around the age of five, or six, or seven, to discover that the flag to which you have pledged allegiance, along with everybody else, has not pledged allegiance to you.

*Flash – we're back in the room with **Elmer**, **George** and **Sheehan**.*

George Merlis   No, I didn't see it.

Buckley   Civil. Proper.

Elmer Lower   But ... ok, Bill, but what makes the whole thing is that it's a conversation, that you're talking to one another.

Buckley   But he is impossible to talk to, with his constant, sly, slithering naughtiness.

George Merlis   You're both getting equally good coverage, Mr Buckley – look.

Buckley   But was I getting equal *time*? It is in my contract, equal time to speak, it sure as hell felt like he was rambling on more than I was.

William Sheehan   We'll make sure Howard is aware.

Buckley *sighs, and heads to –*

The soundstage again, for 'Round 2'. **Vidal** *already here, ready, beaming.*

Howard K. Smith   Now, what I know many of you out there are returning here for tonight. How the English language ought to be used by two craftsmen, our guest commentators: William F. Buckley Jr. And Gore Vidal.

Mr Vidal?

Vidal   Tonight the key question for every patriot is can an ageing Hollywood juvenile actor with a right-wing script defeat Richard Nixon, a professional politician, who currently represents no discernible interest except his own.

Buckley *sighs, immediately off guard, but breathes.*

Buckley   If I may say so, Mr Smith. We were treated to Mr Gore Vidal, the playwright, saying that after all Ronald Reagan was nothing more than a quote, 'ageing Hollywood juvenile actor'. Now to begin with, everyone is ageing ...

Smith *laughs.*

Uh, even Mr Vid–

Vidal (*cutting in first*)   Even you are Bill, perceptibly before our eyes ...

Buckley   Yeah, therefore, that adjective didn't contribute anything extraordinary to the human understanding.

Then he said 'Hollywood'. Now, Mr Vidal sends all of his books to Hollywood, many of which are rejected, but some of which –

Vidal   Now Bill, I don't send any there.

Buckley   My point is –

Vidal   Yes, get to it.

Buckley   If – ... if you play this sort of game you can say 'look, I don't think it's right to present Mr Gore Vidal as a political commentator of any consequence since he is nothing more than a literary producer of perverted Hollywood-minded prose'.

Vidal   Now, now Bill ... careful now.

Buckley   I'm almost through.

Vidal   Hah. In every sense.

Howard K. Smith   Let Mr Buckley finish –

Vidal   As usual, Mr Buckley ... with his enormous, and thrilling charm ... manages to get away from the issue towards comedy.

One of **Buckley**'s *largest of eyerolls, as* **Vidal** *refers to his clipboard prep.*

Vidal   He is always to the right, I think, and almost always in the wrong. And you certainly must your bloodthirsty reputation, Bill, as the Marie Antoinette of the right-wing.

Buckley   Mr Smith, I was invited here and I am prepared to try and talk about the Republican Convention ...

Howard K. Smith   Yes.

Buckley   … but I maintain that it's very difficult to do so when you have somebody like this, who speaks in such burps, and who likes to be 'naughty'. Which has proved a highly merchandisable vice.

Vidal   Not unlike your so public vices –

Buckley   No I don't have any public vices –

Vidal   … and wickedness, Bill.

Frank Meyer   Stop there.

We find ourselves now simultaneously in **Buckley**'*s suite, with his team.*

Pre-match analysis, watching the tape back.

Frank Meyer   Wind the tape back.

Buckley   Please, living through it once was tedious enough, I don't see why we have to watch the tapes back again, each time –

Frank Meyer   We're trying to *learn* from them, Bill. To improve. You cannot keep getting pulled into this trap of chasing any quote he pulls from his ass.

Simply say, 'I don't recognise that', and then get back to *your* point.

Patricia Buckley   Also, is that little worm allowed to call on your 'wickedness' on national television? Why didn't Howard step in, it's libellous. The mind boggles.

Frank Meyer   Let's keep watching.

It continues –

Buckley   Mr Vidal, I have no doubt that there is somebody in Haight-Ashbury or Greenwich village who considers your caricature fetching, uh, I don't. And –

Vidal (*mockingly nice*)   I'm so happy to see your elegant prose style at its very best tonight, Bill. It's very inspiring to those of us listening to it.

Buckley (*trying to stay calm*)   I think you're being sarcastic.

Turning back to the room –

See I thought I was doing well here, showing that he couldn't anger me by belittling our publication. A sense of humour? No?

It continues –

Vidal   As Pericles once pointed out, once you get an empire, it's very difficult to let it go. But if we don't let it go it's going to wreck us economically, at a time when the resources should go to the slums and the poor and for trying to revive an extremely shabby country.

Buckley   The country is not quite so shabby as Mr Vidal believes.

Vidal   It'll be shabbier if the Rep–

Buckley   This is the hobgoblinization of the Marxists. But there are left in America people who can penetrate such myths that have been energetically projected by Mr Vidal, and who choose not to avail themselves of the alternative that Mr Vidal offers them up. Which would not only be a philosophy of economic stagnation, but also a spiritual world of stagnation.

Back in the Suite.

Patricia Buckley   Well that was nice. 'A spiritual world of stagnation'. Yes, precisely.

She kisses him, and they hold one another.

You're fighting the good fight, Ducky. And I am very proud. Whatever anyone else says.

On the other side we find:

Vidal *reclining and drinking with* **Matt**, *and some* **Sycophants**, *and* **George Merlis**.

Sycophant   The 'Marie Antoinette' of the Right!

Laughing.

How did you come up with that on the spot?

Vidal   Well, little secret, sometimes I *may* prepare a few little manoeuvres in advance. I try it out on the producers – George Marketing, I tried that one out on you, didn't I, Young George?

George Merlis   You did, yes.

Matt   And *me*. I laughed.

Vidal   And actually (*leading* **George** *off privately,* **Matt** *watching*), George, some observations on the format having watched the playbacks. I don't think it works, the director cutting to Bill when *I'm* speaking. It's something about the language of television that we're all learning – my words are suddenly seen through the prism of his reaction. It alters the *meaning* of my words. Do you see?

George Merlis   I, uh … sure, I'll have a word and see what I can –

Vidal   There's a good man.

Matt   Everything alright?

Vidal (*returning*)   We were just noting how grotesque it is to have that man's face on camera when *I* am talking.

Sycophant   He certainly has some peculiarities, doesn't he!

Vidal   You mean this?

Mocks his smile.

Sycophant   Yes! His smile!

Vidal   It's as though one side of his mouth decided to enjoy something without telling the other!

Matt   It's his eyes. (*Imitates.*) The blinking!

Vidal   And then his tongue. (*Imitates.*) Yurk! I want to tell him to stick it back in his cheek the whole time. In fact (*clicking at* **Matt** *to write that down*), I shall!

More laughter.

Buckley *reappears.* **Vidal** *clocks him.*

They circle one another. Back to –

The soundstage.

In their seats, waiting.

Vidal   Well. Final day in Miami.

Where did they put you, by the way?

Buckley   The Four Seasons.

Vidal   Mm. I'm at the St Regis.

Buckley   I didn't ask.

William Sheehan   Ready? And five … four …

Lights.

Howard K. Smith   We would now like to call upon our two 'controversialists'. That's a term from the BBC in London, and it's a good one. I beg our guests to look beyond the nomination.

Vidal   Well, Richard Nixon, if he's the candidate, and we assume he will be in a very few minutes … I think it would be an absolute disaster because the young, the Black, the poor are disaffected and I don't see him ever drawing them to him.

Buckley   Well, yeah, well –

Vidal   We have a 75 billion military budget. We have *two billion* dollars for poverty.

Buckley   If you get us nice and socialised like India then we'll all be poor.

Vidal   Does it appeal to you that in the United States, 5 per cent of the population have 20 per cent of the income, and the *bottom* 20 per cent have 5 per cent of the income?

Buckley   I think this is irrelevant.

Vidal   This seems to me … I know that you revel in a kind of inequality.

Buckley   No, I think it's / sort of because …

Vidal   Because then this / is based upon that –

Buckley   You see, I believe that freedom breeds inequality.

Vidal   Say that again?

Buckley   Freedom – breeds – inequality, now I'll say it a Third Time –

Vidal   No, twice is enough. / I think you made your points, yes.

Buckley   Unless you have freedom to be unequal there is no such thing as freedom. And that we ought to encourage a system that permits people like you, and people like Mr Smith, and people like –

Sitting up higher now, gesturing a littler wilder, taking in the room.

– like the technicians and the people in this room to Make Progress. The fact that they make more progress than Other People is not their fault, nor is it the fault of other people. It's the fault of freedom.

Vidal   Don't agree.

Buckley   I think the strongest line Mr Nixon could take is to face the people of the United States and say, 'The principal reason, for the discontentment of our time, is because you have been encouraged by a demagogy of the left to believe that the federal government is going to take care of your life for you.'

The answer is the federal government a) can't, b) shouldn't, c) won't.

Under the circumstances, look primarily to your own resources – spiritual, economic, and philosophical – and don't look to the government to do it because the government is going to fail you.

Buckley *leans back, trying to rein in his passion a little, as* **Vidal** *sighs.*

Vidal   Well, what can I say?

Buckley   Not much.

Vidal   You have given that ghastly position once again.

Buckley   Yeah.

Vidal   Of the well-to-do and those who inherit money and believe that others who do not –

Buckley (*looking to* **Smith** *and the producers*) You know, this is such *balderdash* –

Vidal   But in actual fact, you are going to have a revolution if you don't give the people what they want.

Buckley*'s finger goes to his lips again, eyes wide, keeping things in.*

Vidal   Now, I'm putting it to your own self-interest, they are going to come and take it away from you.

Buckley   Listen, my friend –

Vidal *laughs.*

Buckley   Mr Vidal, if you really believe that the way to address the people of the United States is to say to them, 'Unless we give you precisely what you want, you are entitled to come and take it, to burn down the buildings, to loot the stores, to disrespect the law'. Then I say you do not recognise that you are an agent for the end of democratic government.

Vidal   And you are the minority position in politics in the country.

Buckley   I believe in America.

Howard K. Smith   We are –

Vidal   Which America?

Howard K. Smith   Can we – can we stop on the words
'Which America'?

Vidal *laughs. But* **Buckley** *is not laughing.*

Vidal   'Which America', very good.

Howard K. Smith   Thank you gentlemen. I hadn't
designed that by the way. In any case you'll be back, I am
delighted to know, when we pick up with the Democrats, in
Chicago.

The lights go out.

Buckley *tries to leave at speed again, forever hampered by his mic
leads.*

He joins **Patricia** *for an end of bout hug, with* **Vidal** *joining*
Matt.

Elmer Lower *arrives, handing out cigars.*

Elmer Lower   Just wonderful! It's all anyone is talking
about! We're up two million on last Convention. Two!
And it'll only climb higher! Nixon just won the Republican
nomination by 92 per cent! While the Democrats are
completely split without Bobby. We've got a real presidential
race on our hands! A nail biter!

He goes. With **Vidal** *and* **Matt** *briefly.*

Vidal   Oh Christ, can it be true? They just united around
a political heavyweight, while our side are about to start
tearing chunks out of one another?

Matt   It's gonna be ok. Come on.

He leads him off.

Buckley   … 'Which America.'

Patricia *enters with telephone.*

Buckley   Hello?

… Uh yes, hello. Mr Nixon, hi. Congratulations on the nomination, sir. I …

Oh, is that so? (*Looking at his wife.*) I hadn't realised that delegates and, and the candidates themselves were taking any notice of …

Chicago? Yes, we'll be going head-to-head again. I'll certainly try my best. For you and – and the movement. Goodbye.

He hangs up. A moment.

I don't believe it. This has actually become a thing. People are watching. The Party's … listening to me …

(*Deep breath.*) This wasn't meant to become so … important. With someone like that, so dangerous sat opposite me, and this format, so unpredictable, and …

We have to get to work. I need to be ready, in Chicago … I have to win, whatever that means, and not just narrowly, not just the 'perception', I need to completely and utterly end his tranche of reckless thought. And obliterate him.

Patricia Buckley   I did warn you, Bill. 'The soul of America'. Remember?

Buckley (*as this sinks in*)   … *Shit.*

Lights down.

Act Two

Scene One – 'Chicago'

The 'Donkey' symbol of the Democrat Party lights up with a ting somewhere, replacing the elephant.

Aretha Franklin *is hit by a spotlight, singing the National Anthem, with her own soulful twist.*

Aretha Franklin

O say can you see, by the dawn's early light,
What so proudly we hailed at the twilight's last gleaming,
Whose broad stripes and bright stars through the
perilous fight,
O'er the ramparts we watched, were so gallantly
streaming?

The sounds of police, their batons against shields, and encroaching sirens begins to drown them out.

And the rocket's red glare, the bombs bursting in air,
Gave proof through the night that our flag was still there;
O say does that star-spangled banner yet wave
O'er the land of the free and the home of the brave?

Backstage. The hulking figure of **Mayor Daley**, *a Chicago bruiser, entering with his Democratic entourage.*

Mayor Daley   Well that's the last mother fucking thing we needed, God dammit. Whose dumb shit idea was that?

Northern Delegate   Mister Mayor, it's Aretha Franklin. The Republicans don't have Aretha Franklin –

Mayor Daley   The Republicans aren't split down the goddamn middle. Did we know she was going to sing it like that? Jazz it up, 'soul sister'.

Northern Delegate   It was her own interpretation –

Southern Delegate   The National Anthem doesn't need an 'interpretation'!

Mayor Daley   Listen to that! Southern Delegates yelling, Northern Delegates cheering. No more! Chicago is my town – my Convention.

As **Elmer Lower** *and* **William Sheehan** *are passing –*

Mayor Daley   And you news boys better know which side your bread is buttered.

Elmer Lower   Mr Mayor?

Mayor Daley   Just keep the cameras pointing in the right direction, ok – don't be broadcasting any trouble from a vocal minority out there on these streets.

Elmer Lower   Cameras can only show what's there, Daley. If protestors *do* descend onto your streets –

Mayor Daley   Bullshit. You pick and you choose. You create 'narratives'. And you say protestors, I say rioters. Well any arsonists clutching a molotov cocktail? I've just issued a new police order. 'Shoot to kill'. Ok?

William Sheehan   Shoot to … ? Jesus Christ, most of these are kids –

Mayor Daley   You do your jobs, the police do theirs, and hopefully the dumb fucking delegates will do theirs too and nominate Humphrey as LBJ's successor. Nice and easy, down the centre. Alright?

(*As he's going.*) Oh, and keep Gore Fucking Vidal on a leash too! He's meant to be one of ours!

Elmer Lower   Gore is not an ABC employee, Daley, he says whatever he likes –

Mayor Daley   For fuck's … we need a convention free of controversy. Vidal is a notorious, narcissistic controversialist. Jesus Christ, why don't you just hand the Republicans the keys to the White House now!

Mayor Daley *steps out onto –*

The Democrat Convention stage.

Mayor Daley   Welcome Delegates! Chicago is delighted to have you.

And rest assured, as long as I'm Mayor of this town … there'll be law and order in Chicago.

Beyond the hall / in the hotel, the Buckley Team might arrive, luggage et al like last time, from one side, and the Gore Team another.

In the **Vidal** *suite. He has congratulatory flowers and cards with him.*

The phone is ringing off the hook, **Matt** *trying to sort everything.*

Vidal (*feigning despair*)   Oh the bells, the bells. (*Then, happily.*) May they never stop.

Matt   Yes, one moment please. (*To* **Vidal**.) It's Norman.

Vidal   Which Norman? Mailer? Add him to the callback list – but gently, now, remember he has been known to stab people.

Matt   Mr – Mr Mailer? Yes, he'll call you back. Ok. (*Phone down.*) He says go fuck yourself you can of intellectual toxic waste.

Vidal   Well, I would fuck myself (*at his watch*), but I've got others to fuck first. I don't want to be too tired. There's Hubert Humphrey for a start, likely nominee but Vietnam Hawk. Then there's the entire Republican Party watching from home and thirsting for my blood …

Matt (*with the letters*)   Everyone is sending notes and leaving messages, Joan Didion. Gloria Steinham. Allen Ginsberg. Arthur Miller and Paul Newman have turned up, they'll be rooting for you on the floor of the convention hall –

Vidal   They're delegates, here to select a nominee, let's not get carried away.

Matt   You're allowed to enjoy it, Gore. I would. I've never – I *will* never have any kind of recognition like this. A platform of this scale.

Vidal   You don't know that.

Matt   I know you're happy. Admit it. From the biggest talker in town, to being the talk *of* the town –

Vidal   I don't need a psychologist.

Matt   Oh then fuck, what do you need? Huh? What *does* Gore Vidal need?

Vidal, *about to answer, or not, when we hear off – some old-school warbled singing.*

Howard Austen   'You always hurt the one you love

The one you shouldn't hurt at all … '

Howard Austen *arrives, grinning. A large man,* **Vidal**'s *age.*

Vidal   And they say *I* am guilty of theatrics.

Howard Austen   ' … You always take the sweetest rose

And crush it till the petals fall … '

Surprise.

Vidal   Not really, I predicted it entirely.

They kiss, lightly on the cheek. **Matt** *not sure where to put himself.*

Vidal   You didn't have to come, Howard. But I'm so glad you did.

Howard Austen   And who do we have here?

Matt   Oh, no one –

Howard Austen   No one is no one.

Matt   Matt, Matthew, hello – I, I'm just helping out with –

Howard Austen   Howard Austen (*shakes*). Gore and I are –

Matt   I know.

Howard Austen   Oh, you do; Christ tell me then, I've never been able to work it out.

Vidal   Howard don't be slinky. I'm afraid I have dinner with three congressman, two senators and one soul singer. I must finish getting ready.

Briefly departs. **Howard** *already making himself a drink. To* **Matt**.

Howard Austen   Please don't squirm, it's alright. Part of the arrangement.

Matt   Ah. I wasn't, erm …

Howard Austen   Well I assume it is. That's the nature of such things, one doesn't put words to them, it's never spoken out loud.

(*Drinks, watching where* **Vidal** *stepped out.*) The funny thing about Gore, a man so verbose; there are things he cannot or will not put words to.

He's never actually said he's a true friend of Dorothy, or even her casual acquaintance. Labels are *declasse* to him. I wouldn't have known what *declasse* was had Gore not picked me up from some bath house twenty-odd years ago.

Matt   So what do you say? To people?

Howard Austen   To people? To press? To the parents who no longer speak to him (*Shrugs.*) That we made a decision to live together forever. What more is there to say?

Vidal *returns.*

Matt   I'll finish up these notes, for … and leave you to it. (*Exits.*)

Howard Austen   Look at this suite!

Vidal (*taking in the view*)   Yes. To the Windy City, from the Miami Seas. You know they're holding this convention in the meatpacking district? Flies everywhere.

Austen   All those armed soldiers, outside. It felt like entering a police state.

Vidal   Matt says the world and his wife are coming here to protest. Black Panthers, Students, anti-Vietnam. Every grievance on earth, and the whole city seems to be holding its breath. Perhaps the entire country, I don't know.

Have you come to drag me back to Italy? Please say it's so.

Howard Austen   Fuck off. Wild horses couldn't, and so on. This is all you've ever wanted.

Vidal   Oh, you're just like him. Go on then, what? You men who know me so well; what has been my soul's desire, now fulfilled? Fame? I already had that.

Howard Austen   You had infamy. This is different. More than that.

(*Arms over his shoulder.*) 'Political significance'. The powerful are taking note. But here's the thing, Gore Vidal. (*Whispering in his ear.*) I think you're better than this. Buckley's right, about you. You –

Vidal   Excuse me? 'Buckley' doesn't have the first damn –

Howard Austen   You're exceptional at being naughty, fine, ok. But where's the writer, the great thinker I know? The great *poet*?

Vidal   Poet?

Howard Austen   Yeah. Poet.

Vidal   So your advice to me is 'be better'; that's incredibly helpful, thank you.

Howard Austen   Why not? Buckley will be better; he's not stupid. He will be, Gore, this time.

(*Drinks.*) You can make them laugh. Hurrah. What about making them think. Making them *feel*. Find the *words* ... to tell them all exactly where we are.

Vidal *checks his watch again, late for his glad-handing. He sighs – accepting they must work.*

The **Buckley** *suite – his team prepping.* **Buckley** *exhausted, closes a book hard.*

Buckley   Good heavens, honestly! Every excruciating essay of his it has been my misfortune to read this past fortnight indicates the real weakness of the new, modern left.

Everything they obsess over and advocate for now actually alienates those who *used* to vote them into power. Normal, hard-working, men and women.

Frank Meyer   It's because the Left don't *care* about class anymore.

Buckley   Exactly! Their obnoxious leaders – Vidal included – aren't now *from* these neighbourhoods, they don't know these people, they probably don't particularly like them. Well, that's a whole new constituency that we can move to our side at last. These are ...

... the 'silent majority', in America.

Frank Meyer   That's exactly who you must speak to, Bill. The 'Silent Majority'.

Buckley   This army of mutinous young people we're told are about to lay siege to this city and wail about how awful American capitalism is. Who are they? Everyday citizens? Hell no! The long-haired college elite. Well, their campus language won't cut through the cameras to Middle America, and so ours must and can and will –

Patricia Buckley   Oh sure, because you sound like a regular trucker at a bar, Bill.

Frank Meyer   Now-now, Bill can be – apple pie –

Buckley   No she's right, I can't. And nor do I desire to. But it's about what I say, not how I say it.

Patricia Buckley   Well this is all well and good, but you're playing the ball. Did the debates in Miami not teach you anything? People are tuning in to watch you play the man.

Buckley   I won't stoop to his –

Patricia Buckley   Bill, listen to me. You're too damn smart. And it is going to kill you out there. The average American as you call them cannot follow all that you're saying, they just can't. So what they are trying to work out instead, between you and Vidal – is who is the better person. And in so doing, whose America they want to live in. His, or yours.

That's it. That's all this is. 'Who do I *like* the most'? And I don't care if Frank disagrees, he's too damn smart too.

Frank Meyer   I agree with everything she's saying.

Buckley   So go on then, Ducky, do tell. How do I beat him in this disgusting popularity contest you are envisioning?

Patricia Buckley   How can you beat him if you don't know him?

She holds out a book for him.

Buckley (*takes it, looks, scoffs*)   Absolutely not.

Frank Meyer   What?

Buckley (*disdainfully*)   'Myra Breckinridge'. The darkest recesses of Vidal's filthy mind.

Patricia Buckley   What, are you worried you might enjoy it?

Buckley   What I would like … is to destroy his character, yes, but to preferably preserve my own. I want to demonstrate you can win the argument, without plumbing his undignified depths.

Patricia Buckley Bi-i-i-ll ...

Buckley Alright, feel free to drag up anything you can about him, so that we can warn America. Who the hell is he? What emotional buttons can I push? What buried trauma is there? Didn't daddy love him, is he a closet Republican acting out of self-loathing, did he lose a cat as a child and if so – what was its name.

Frank Meyer I know some people at his publishers. I could pump them for intel.

Patricia Buckley I have the gays covered. You know, I think quite a few of them might loathe him more than we do.

And Bill?

She holds out the book again. He reluctantly takes it with a groan.

In the streets of Chicago ...

Protestors The Whole World is Watching! The Whole World is Watching!

The **Protestors** *and their whistle and drums suddenly morph into ...*

... Police, banging riot shields.

... Suddenly some of the police officers snap into lip-sync interviewers –

David Huntley Paul Newman?

Paul Newman 'All this security makes me very nervous. But it's necessary, apparently.'

Arthur Miller 'It's a little frightening quite frankly, being in this fortress. Trying to select a president.'

Protestors 'The Whole World is Watching! The Whole World is Watching!'

The Buckley team, surrounded by research.

Frank Meyer He grew up in D.C. No one grows up in Washington, D.C. It's a swamp you travel *to*, in order to do politics. But Gore Vidal, as I live and breathe ... No wonder he's so sycophantic about Government Power.

Patricia Buckley   Parents divorced.

Buckley   Naturally.

Frank Meyer   He moved from house to house, mainly with his grandfather.

Buckley   This is the blind Senator.

Frank Meyer   He ran for Congress.

Buckley   And lost.

Patricia Buckley   You lost, when you ran for Mayor.

Buckley   Yes thank you dear, and that's different, I was running disingenuously. He was sincere.

Patricia Buckley   Ah.

Frank Meyer It was at the same time his pal John F. Kennedy was running for the Senate. Only Gore lost.

Buckley (*an idea*)   Yes. Yes in fact, wait a minute, wait a minute ... (*searching his files*)

Patricia Buckley   What are you looking for?

Buckley   A letter. A silver bullet, to load into my pistol. It's here somewhere ...

He loathes the mention of any of the Kennedys – it disorientates him, why? They all got what he truly wants but pretends otherwise. He's an outsider, desperate to be 'in'.

Patricia Buckley   So are you.

Buckley   I am not.

Patricia Buckley   Hah. Look at you. No wonder you loathe one another, you're the same people.

Buckley We are not the same. I think that's self-evident.

Patricia Buckley Two sides of the same coin, then.

Buckley Pff.

Patricia Buckley (*back to her reading*) He has *two* apartments in Italy. Ravello, and Rome. A place in New York. Another in LA. And a long-term 'something' with this Howard Austen fellow, though whatever it is exactly, the one thing it isn't is monogamous.

Buckley Goodness he really can't make up his mind, can he.

Patricia Buckley Not only that, he doesn't even go by his 'real' name. His Christian name is Eugene. Gore isn't even a Christian name, it's a surname he just took it and gave it to himself.

Buckley (*pacing*) … My God. He doesn't even exist, does he. Nothing about him is real, permanent. He has no roots. He doesn't *come* from anywhere. He has no regular *family*. He is incapable of committing to a *relationship* as much as he is a *country* to reside in.

No wonder he wants to burn it all down and to hell with the consequences. He lives an entirely consequence – free life …

Gore *paces, reading from the* National Review.

Vidal 'Though liberals do a great deal of talking about hearing other points of view, it sometimes shocks them to learn that there *are* other points of view.'

(*Considers this.*) Hmm. (*Before carrying on …*)

Frank and **Buckley** *are on their feet – 'training' as though about to enter a boxing bout.*

Frank Meyer So, new tactics. You have to come out strong as soon as the bell rings. Vidal will likely do what he did in Miami, go immediately below the belt –

Patricia Buckley   – by saying something provocative and personal, a punch to the gut to wobble you. Instead –

Buckley   I block that, and back off –

Patricia Buckley   – *enjoying* the insult. Bill, you need to revel in his pastiche of you as the Arch Conservative. Laugh it off. Hahaha.

Buckley   'Hahahaha.'

Patricia Buckley   And then surprise him by –?

Frank Meyer   Going in for a 'clinch'. Saying something he agrees with. (*Hug.*)

Buckley   Ugh, just the thought.

Frank Meyer   But he's confused. He clinches back. Agreeing with *you*. And that's when you counter, with an uppercut – pow!

Patricia Buckley   – getting personal back, attacking his character. He's disorientated, 'where did that come from?!'– So he swings wildly. He looks deranged. You back off –

Frank Meyer   And while he's flailing around, confused that his left jabs aren't connecting, you come in with a Straight Right Counter –

Buckley (*does a punch*)   Common sense. (*Another.*) Principled. (*Another.*) Practical.

Patricia Buckley   Yes, you've got him on the ropes, now!

Frank Meyer   Time some low blows of your own!

Buckley (*low blows*)   Lives abroad, hates America, pervert –

Frank Meyer   And he's down!

Arms in the air from all.

Music! Dance!

Myra Breckinridge   I am Myra Breckinridge, whom no man will ever possess. The new woman whose astonishing history started with a surgeon's scalpel, and will end ... who knows where.

She dances and gyrates, dominatrix-style, over **Buckley**.

Myra Breckinridge   Who is Myra Breckinridge? What is she? Myra Breckinridge is a dish, and don't you ever forget it, you motherfuckers ... As the children say nowadays.

Buckley *paces away from this, privately now, reading from* Myra Breckinridge.

Myra Breckinridge   My mission: the destruction of the last vestigial traces of traditional manhood ...

Buckley   Oh heavens.

Myra Breckinridge   ... in the race to realign the sexes, thus reducing population, while increasing human happiness and preparing humanity for its next – stage.

Vidal   Of course, you know my theory. Why does any bigot really hate the gays so much? (*Grinning.*)

Howard Austen   Oh come off it, such a cliché.

Matt   He is very – effete.

Howard Austen   He's rich. Rich and gay often look the same.

Vidal   I don't know. I do – not – know. Useful buttons to push though as we hit Round Two.

Scene Two

Howard K. Smith *introduces them from his desk.*

As around about so too each of the 'teams' – **Patricia**, **Howard Austen**, *and so on – willing them on and reacting to hits and misses ...*

Howard K. Smith After their successful debut as convention commentators in Miami Beach, William F. Buckley, the Conservative commentator on the defensive in Miami, may now take the offensive. But I beg to put the question to Gore Vidal, author, playwright, increasingly also a commentator. Mr Vidal, do you feel more comfortable philosophically here than you did in Miami?

Vidal *starting carefully ...*

Vidal 'Philosophically.' I wonder if that word will ever be used again while we're here in Chicago. This place – is a shambles, a police state. One's aware of the horrors of the world here, the smell of old blood, the shrieking of pigs as they are slaughtered in the morning. All this reminds one of life and death.

Howard Austen Lovely, calm, 'gravitas'.

Vidal And I think the conversations that are going on now ... seem to be particularly *urgent*. In a sense I do feel at home in a way. But not happy.

That had more 'weight' than normal – **Matt***, watching, pats* **Howard***.*

Matt Good, nice.

Howard K. Smith Mr Buckley, what do you think will be the main weaknesses the Democrats will display here in convention assembled?

Buckley For years, America has elected a Democratic President, a Democratic Senate, a Democratic House, but what has been done to greatly speed America along its way? To achieve stability, or security?

I think the main weakness of the party at this point is the collision between its ideology, and the Practical Consequences of its ideology.

A party that preaches 'peace', and leaves the world periodically in shambles. The uncertain war in Vietnam, the politics of unrealism in Europe …

Frank Meyer   Come on, Bill, remember the plan, something he can agree on.

Buckley   The fact the Democratic plank commits to, quote, 'encourage by all peaceful means the growing independence of the captive peoples living under communism …'. If in fact America can't devise a foreign policy that seeks to affect these goals, why do they bother to create the rhetoric?

Howard K. Smith   Mr Vidal?

Vidal *is briefly wrongfooted – taking a moment.*

Vidal   … I think that's an awfully good question. I'm happy to see you doing your homework, Bill, that you quote from the platform of the Democrats. I think … I quite agree, it is totally irrelevant rhetoric … and I wish we'd stop it.

Frank Meyer   Now, in for the kill –

Buckley   Except *you* specialise in looking crises in the face and saying irrelevant things about how impossible it is to do anything about them. The Republicans specialise in avoiding crises. Have you noticed that we haven't had any major wars when the Republicans are in? Or have you not done *your* homework?

Vidal   I – I – if I may say so, no thanks to you. Because you, after all, favoured the invasion of Cuba, which –

Buckley   The invasion of Cuba was undertaken by a *Democratic* administration.

Vidal   … Y– …

Frank Meyer   Hah!

Vidal *tries to reclaim the initiative.*

Vidal   Mr Buckley really does believe in these Holy Wars, that we are the forces of light, and they are night. Forcing ourselves upon the world. To what end? (*Losing his cool, now.*) To what end?!

Buckley   It seems you know less about international politics than even I supposed. The reason, Mr Vidal, is because there is among Decent People ... (*Looks directly at him.*)

... a tradition that dates back to the Declaration of Independence that says we have a concern for the decent opinion of mankind.

Vidal   We have lost the good opinion of all decent men in Europe –

Buckley   No.

Vidal   – most of our traditional allies, of Canada. We've lost in Vietnam –

Buckley (*laughing*)   'We've lost Canada'?

Howard K. Smith   We have about / twenty seconds –

Buckley   And it is also true, that some people lose respect for you precisely at the moment when you should be *earning* their respect.

Incredibly pointed, at **Vidal***, who flusters.*

A bell rings, and we just forward to –

The soundstage again, cameras rolling. The next day's debate.

Buckley *even more assured than before, enjoying himself, unlike –*

Buckley   The important difference is the Democrats are clearly displeased with their own plank, whereas the Republican's represents the overwhelming majority of them.

Looks to **Vidal**, *smiling*.

Vidal … I, I think that's well observed. The Republicans are pretty united. I accept, there is a definite split here.

I personally favour, as many people do, the McCarthy/ McGovern Vietnam plank over Hubert Humphrey's proposals –

Buckley (*removing his silver bullet*) Perhaps as a matter of testamentary integrity, I could reveal a concrete proposal contained in a letter sent to me by the late Senator Kennedy about six months ago, the P.S of which was: 'Instead of giving blood to the Vietcong, we should give them Gore Vidal.'

Vidal (*grinning, in disbelief*) May I see that? *Really?*

Buckley *happily hands it over.*

Buckley I do share Mr Kennedy's notion that Mr Vidal's idea of how to prosecute the whole situation out there is marred by his sort of strange fantasies concerning the realism of politics.

Vidal I must say, I am looking at this. What very curious handwriting. It also slants up. Sign of a manic depressive. Well, whether you forged it or not, I don't know.

Buckley *laughs.*

Vidal I will have to have my handwriting experts, the graphologists will have to take a look at it. I put nothing beyond you. The fact that he was writing you letters makes me terribly suspicious of him as a presidential candidate. But to get back to the plank – … it's been fun inspecting your correspondence.

Buckley *laughs. We snap to later –*

Buckley Now wait a minute –

Vidal   We have nothing to gain by this war!

Buckley   We have *not* lost the war in Vietnam, what we *have* lost … is an opportunity to press that war with such weapons that are especially at our disposal.

Vidal   Do you favour an all-out war on Communism?

Buckley   No –

Vidal   To use nuclear weapons as you / have … in the past, on … ?

Buckley   No, Mr Vidal, I never said … I / never said –

Howard K. Smith   You are both much better when you don't talk at the same time. / Could we take turns?

Vidal   I don't see how Mr Buckley, with his concerted will, thinks that we're going to win a war that we have spent certainly five aggressive years in losing. / Now I assume –

Buckley   I said we *could* win … I didn't say we were going to.

Vidal   You said we *will* win.

Buckley (*sitting up, emphatically*)   I said we *could*. Mr Vidal.

Vidal   Could we or should we?

Buckley   Oh, well, obviously, we should.

Vidal   A-ha, well, that's all we needed to know. Here he sits, take a good look at the leading warmonger of the United States! Bill, don't point your tongue at me now. Keep it in your cheek where it belongs.

Buckley   If I am the leading warmonger in the United States then I am contrasted with you in the sense in which the majority of people of the United States – including the leadership of the Democratic Party and the leadership of the Republican Party – belong with *me*, while you, uh, (*grinning*) go to Rome and expatriate yourself –

Vidal   Oh I think we need to straighten this out now. I don't expatriate myself. I have an apartment in Rome and I go there for two or three months every year to be close to the Vatican to contemplate William Buckley, and his mad activities back here, with enormous serenity.

Buckley   Well, the encyclopaedia of morality which constitutes *your* published work is hardly *my* primary source.

Vidal   Do you read? You could learn a great deal.

Howard K. Smith   Mr Vidal –

Vidal   I think, to be perfectly bleak and to be perfectly blunt, I think we're headed for total disaster, this empire. With people like Mr Buckley here, beating the drum.

The ecological balance of the planet is upset. The food supply is in danger. I think there is war coming.

Buckley   Mr Smith, this is a recurrent phenomenon. People who like to sort of massage their world-weariness and tell us how everything is going to the dogs. There's a curious coincidence about the fact that it's always going to the dogs because we don't do what *they* tell us to do.

Vidal   Well, as a matter of fact, this year's liberal rhetoric *has* fallen into a Conservative chapter. It's all about private enterprise making money, not doing good –

Buckley   Don't you understand, Mr Vidal, that the Making of Money is, according to systems discovered 300 years ago, a way of helping people because it is a way of making goods available to people at a cheaper price. Got it? Got it?

Howard K. Smith   I think this is the last remark. Can you do it in one line?

Vidal   Yes, simply in one line, it has been a great pleasure to observe America's leading hawk and great heart with enormous compassion – *don't* stick your tongue out, Bill … once again in action … (*faltering*) …

Howard K. Smith   That was a long line. We must break it off there and continue tomorrow night.

Lights turn – bells ring – the men stand.

Buckley *stretches, relaxed.* **Vidal** *gets a little tangled in his mic pack.*

Buckley   Need a hand?

Vidal   No, thank you –

He paces off to **Howard** *and* **Matt***, as* **Buckley** *smiles and watches him go.*

Howard Austen   You did fine.

Vidal   Shut up.

Howard Austen   You did good.

Vidal   Shut up. Just shut the fuck up.

Howard Austen   Look, what's the difference, as usual your supporters will think you did better, his supporters will think he did –

Vidal   That is not enough. That is no longer enough –

Matt   It's not enough, I agree.

Howard Austen   What was with your 'tongue' reference, over and over –

Vidal   He threw me, I –

Howard Austen   Gore, you are a chronicler of antiquity, the great biographer of America, enough with the stupid goddamn jibes –

Matt   You could walk out. I would. Just refuse to be here.

Howard Austen   That's not very grown up, Matthew.

Matt   The whole Convention is a stitch up, a sham. Real politics is happening on the streets. You should want to be *outside*, Gore –

Howard Austen   And what would that look like? Leaving the field?

Matt   I know the advice you're going to be given, and that you'll probably take out of pride. 'Be less angry, less loud, more like Him'. When you should be angrier, louder, like the people out there –

Howard Austen   The people Out There are going to hand this election to the Republicans, who won't deliver any of what they want.

Matt   Well at least they're honest.

Vidal   Enough! Ok, enough fucking advice, Jesus Christ I just, I – … I need to *think*.

He exits, to be alone, when suddenly we find:

Aide   Mr Vidal? (*As he looks.*) Might you have a moment?

We snap to –

The Conference Hall. Shouting and chaos.

Mayor Daley *is shaking his fist and jeering at –*

Senator Ribicoff (*from the podium*)   'As I look at the confusion in the Hall. And watch on television the turmoil and violence that is competing with this great Convention, for the attention of the American People. There is something else in my heart tonight. With McGovern as President of the United States, we wouldn't have to have gestapo tactics in the streets. With McGovern, we wouldn't have a National Guard … !'

The Convention explodes, between booing and cheering.

Backstage. With **Vidal** *and the* **Aide**.

Mayor Daley   Those TV bastards! Whose side are they on? East coast pricks. (*To* **Vidal**.) They pointed the camera straight at me, right at me, to capture my response to

Ribicoff pissing on my city from the DNC stage! Your friends at ABC, fucking 'lipreaders', saying that I said – what are they saying I said?

Aide (*reading*)   Uh, 'fuck you, you Jew son of a bitch, you lousy motherfucker, go home.'

Vidal   And that's not what you said?

Mayor Daley   That is *exactly* what I said! But it was my business saying it! We should throw the cameras out of here. Democracy can't function like this!

But you, Gore. Look at you. Flying the flag, every night, doing your bit.

Vidal   Mayor Daley, my positions are quite clear, on the war, and on how you are running this –

Mayor Daley   I only mean … it's great to see you, back in the centre of things. (*A hand on his shoulder.*) I know your journey up through this party was … well, it didn't go how you might have … look what I'm saying is that what I'm *seeing*, what we're all seeing, is the real Gore. A statesman. And I think if you continue fighting for us on air, in your own way, not propagandising, just singing your Own Party's Song, well … maybe there are Senate seats such as that fucker Ribicoff's out there that might become available after all.

Vidal   …

Mayor Daley   Come back inside, Gore. Come in from the cold.

Elsewhere, in the Convention hall, **Elmer** *is reviewing his press and his sales figures.*

Chet Huntley *and* **David Brinkley** *pass.*

Elmer Lower   Well look who it is! Mr Huntley, Mr Brinkley, how goes it at CBS?

David Brinkley   You're looking very much at home in these old stockyards, Elmer, rolling around like a pig in shit.

Elmer Lower   Oh is that so, oh well I'm just going over our ratings. Where *are* all these extra viewers coming from? Oh gosh, I – I sure hope we're not taking them from *you*.

Chet Huntley   Said with all the characteristic grace of your political coverage, I see.

Elmer Lower   Yeah, you know what I see? You two, interviewing celebrities now, putting famous mouthpieces on screen. Don't seem to be laughing at our little experiment quite so much anymore, huh.

Chet Huntley   It's the Democrats for God's sake, all of Hollywood is here, you can't swing without hitting someone famous –

David Brinkley   And believe me, we wouldn't be lowering ourselves if we had any say in it –

Elmer Lower   Lowering yours – … who's lowering themselves? Buckley and Vidal are the smartest men in America, they're elevating the discourse –

David Brinkley (*snapping*)   They're *insulting* each other, Elmer. It's a slanging match. Nothing more. And it's –

Elmer Lower   Nothin– …! Have you even been listening? (*Referencing his sheets of paper.*) Look at what they're *saying*. 'Metaphysical differentialism' … 'Marxist hobgoblinisation' … 'recidivist imperialism'. Recidivist imperialism, on prime-time network television! I don't even know what it fucking means, but these are smart words. Big words. Huge!

Chet Huntley   It's theatre.

Elmer Lower   Well people like theatre; some of it.

Chet Huntley   And I'll be damned if – (*slaps his neck*). Goddamn these flies! What genius decided to hold the convention here? Hogs and cows being slaughtered in the midday heat. It feels prophetic.

David Brinkley   Pathetic?

Chet Huntley   *Pro-phetic.*

David Brinkley   I stand by mine. (*Pointedly, at* **Elmer**.) It's *pathetic.*

They go.

In the Streets of Chicago ...

Protestors   The Whole World is Watching! The Whole World is Watching!

The American Flag.

And a protestor.

Against the sound of mounting riots, she 'climbs' up, with their help of her friends, and replaces the flag with the flag of the Vietcong.

The noise of a growing riot gathering ...

An **ABC Reporter** *arrives with his cameraman.*

Snap – we might catch pockets of footage here – the images of the police gathering, and beating and dragging people off the streets to screams and cries ...

Gore Vidal *is drinking, as* **Matt** *arrives.*

Matt   It's a full-scale riot, downtown – fuck, my eyes.

Vidal   Matthew?

Matt   The police, they're dragging protestors away, they're firing tear gas into the streets.

Vidal   Why? What happened, how did –

Matt   The Mayor's office denied marchers a permit to assemble in the park, but there were already thousands on their way, and then someone took down a flag – I don't know, you need to ask your producers to send more people down there *now*, folks have to see this –

Vidal I'm going down there myself.

Matt Don't be an idiot, you'll be hurt.

Vidal Well maybe I should be.

Matt Gore this is fucking real. It's not a TV show, it …

(*Looking at him now.*) You think you sit there, under those lights, and it's real, that it matters. On the frontline of history. You're nowhere near the frontline, Gore, you never are, any of you. You distance yourself from everything, and everyone …

He leaves. After a beat, **Gore** *follows.*

A 'cloud of tear gas' emerges. It's surreal.

Buckley *is watching from 'above' (in his hotel room), as* **Vidal** *appears below.*

It's strange – almost like a dream – as shadows of protestors and police pass by around him – torches, and flares and …

Both men find themselves in the fog together, facing off against one another.

They grab one another. Rictus with loathing. As they try to overpower each other the cacophony of rioting grows and grows …

In the Convention Hall studio, an **ABC Reporter** *is bundled in, bleeding and eyes bright red, being given assistance by* **William Sheehan** *and* **George Merlis**.

Vidal *and* **Buckley**, *who are being prepped for the final debate, break off and join.*

William Sheehan Are you ok?

Vidal What happened?

ABC Reporter Ah, Jesus, my eyes.

George Merlis The protest is outside the Convention Hall now, they're right at the gates.

Buckley   Are the police lines holding?

George Merlis   They're using tear gas and mace.

Vidal   On reporters?!

Howard K. Smith *arrives with* **Elmer Lower**.

Howard K. Smith (*arriving*)   What on earth is going on? Are you ok? You're bleeding.

ABC Reporter   It's just a bit of a blow to the head, I'm alright.

Howard K. Smith   We can't have our own news teams being beaten by the police. We've up to twenty reporters with injury being caried in here and there's – goddammit (*wafting his script*), there's tear gas spreading into the Hall now.

George Merlis   Maybe it'll help with the flies.

Howard K. Smith   This is the assistant director who got hit in the hand with the bullet that killed Bobby Kennedy! Where's the protection, let alone the respect –

Gore Vidal   … That was you? With Bobby?

ABC Reporter (*shaking hand in pain*)   It's not as bad as it looks. It just hurts a little. Excuse me, I just need a second.

Elmer Lower   Alright, I want everyone in production to wear these masks, ok? And, and we'll put fans on the stage to clear gas that's there, we've got half an hour until the air.

Howard K. Smith   You need to speak to the Mayor, Elmer, this is damned absurd.

Buckley   If I may, Mr Smith, it is not the job of the news to get involved in local politics, merely report it. And those lines of police officers are trying to keep us safe.

Vidal   Are you out of your mind? (*At the bleeding* **Reporter**.) Does *she* look safe?

Buckley   In this hall, there are men and women trying to engage in peaceful democratic action, the same action threatened by an angry revolutionary mob.

Vidal   I wish I was out there with them!

Buckley   Do be my guest.

Elmer Lower   Gentlemen, maybe save it for your final showdown? Everyone else, I want to see masks! We go live in thirty!

Everyone departs with purpose. We follow –

Vidal, *to his own dressing room, taking a breather. Re-touching his own make-up.*

He notices that his hands are shaking …

The familiar sight of **James Baldwin** *appearing quietly, watching, and lighting a cigarette.*

James Baldwin   I do believe that Gore Vidal is scared …

Vidal   I'm not scared, Jimmy. I'm incandescent with rage.

Beat, then:

And – … a little scared.

What is happening? I think we're losing. Are we losing? Am I? The Leadership, they're 'buckling'. Buckling under Buckley and his seemingly unstoppable, advancing Conservatism. Look at what the Mayor is doing, a *liberal* mayor, in a *liberal* city, using the very same language of Law and goddamn Order. It's working, we're, we're moving in their direction, aren't we, moving to the right –

James Baldwin   The Democratic Party?

Vidal   America. I didn't see it. And now –

James Baldwin   The forces of history have driven us to this point. You cannot take the weight of that responsibility on yourself.

Vidal   I volunteered myself into that chair. Thinking it would all be a bit of fun, a nice profile booster; that Buckley would crumple under my ferocious – ... my – ...

It wasn't supposed to matter. Maybe it doesn't, maybe I'm kidding myself, as I always do ...

James Baldwin   You're right. It shouldn't have mattered. This pageant, this pantomime. The problem is ... people like blood sports, and they tuned in. And so now it does matter. Now you have to win.

Vidal   ... How did you beat him? At Cambridge, how?

James Baldwin   Did I beat him?

Vidal   You got the votes.

James Baldwin   Yes, but did I beat him. Look around.

He said the strangest thing to me, just before we began. He asked me if I 'enjoyed' this kind of thing. And I could not fathom what he meant. Did I *enjoy* ... speaking for my life, and the life of millions of others? Did I enjoy a battle for people's right to simply exist, and be heard, and be happy? But of course now I see. The real world, to him, and to others ... possibly if I may say this, to *you* as well ... it's an abstraction. A thing to consider, like a painting, and express a viewpoint on it. But you aren't in it. Maybe I am not in it, anymore. I make my speeches and, don't get me wrong, I think speeches are important. We write our books and our plays, and don't get me wrong, I think they are vital too. For our humanity. We have our – 'debates'. But let's be honest, 'Eugene', you are a god up high on Olympus, musing upon the activities of Man below. As though it were an intellectual curiosity of no significance.

(*Puts his cigarette out.*) Well I'm afraid now there is. We are going to go one way, or the other. And as you say – you put yourself in that chair. And we are where we are.

And the Whole World is Watching ...

A beat. **James** *goes.*

Vidal *takes a breath, before stepping out.*

Through the light smoke, passing ...

ABC Reporter, *the reporter from earlier, still catching his breath. He instinctively raises his hand at the sight of someone coming.* **Vidal** *stops.*

A moment, where **Vidal** *takes the man's raised hand, with the old bullet wound in the centre of it.*

And he places it gently against his face, eyes closed, just briefly ...

The **Reporter** *not sure what to do, as* **Vidal** *removes the hand, and continues on his way.*

On his way, he passes **Mayor Daley**.

Decision made, **Vidal** *offers the middle-finger to him, and his offer. Continuing on, to –*

The ABC soundstage.

The bizarre sight of many production staff wearing gas masks. Electric fans are cleared from the soundstage, as **Buckley** *and* **Vidal** *arrive.*

The studio is full, tensions high, all eyes on them as they prepare and sit.

They both look angry, *holding it in.*

William Sheehan   Five ...

Howard K. Smith *arrives at his desk.*

William Sheehan   Four ...

Buckley *and* **Gore** *shift in their seats, getting ready.*

William Sheehan   Three ... two ...

The lights change. And we begin.

Howard K. Smith   To our two guest commentators,
William Buckley and Gore Vidal, and to ask them what
observations they've made about the security that we have
seen all week this convention, and the events tonight on the
streets beyond this convention hall.

Who is first?

Mr Vidal, first?

A moment.

Vidal   I think there is very little that we can say that would
be in any way adequate. It's like living under a Soviet
regime here. The guards, the soldiers, the *agents provocateur*
on the parts of the police. You've seen the roughing up. It
was a friendly, nonviolent demonstration.

Buckley *writes a note down.*

As a rule the press is on the side of the police. But this time
the police have seriously injured twenty-one newsmen, and
the press has, of course, reacted …

Howard K. Smith   I wonder if we can let Mr Buckley
comment now for a short while.

Buckley   The distinctions to be made, Mr Smith, are these.
Number One, do we have enough evidence to indict a large
number of individual Chicago policemen? It would seem
from what *you* have shown us that we do.

However. The effort here – not only on your program
tonight, but during the past two or three days in Chicago –
has been to 'institutionalise' this complaint; that, in effect,
we have got a police state going on here, we have got a sort
of fascist situation.

The point is that policeman violate their obligations just the
way politicians do.

Vidal   The point –

Buckley (*voice rising*)   And if we could all work up an equal sweat, and if you all would be obliging enough to have your cameras handy every time a politician commits demagogy, or passes along graft or bribes, or every time a labour union beats up people who refuse to join his union, then maybe we could work up some kind of impartiality in resentment. But don't do what's happening here in Chicago tonight, which is to infer from individual and despicable acts of violence, a case for implicit totalitarianism in the American system.

He sits back again. Done.

Howard K. Smith   Mr Vidal.

Vidal   We have the right, according to our Constitution, of freedom of assembly. These people came here with no desire other than anybody's ever been able to prove, than to hold peaceful demonstration.

Buckley   I can prove it.

*Their first interaction in this debate, **Vidal** cutting in quick, but held-in and calm.*

Vidal   How can you prove it?

Buckley   Very easily. I was fourteen windows above that gang last night. These sweet little girls with their sun-baked dresses that we heard described a moment ago, and the chant between 11 o'clock and 5 o'clock this morning, some four or five thousand voices, was sheer and utter obscenities directed at the President of the United States, at the Mayor of this City … this is their way of accosting American Society. And I say it is *remarkable* that there was as much restraint shown as was shown, for instance, last night, by cops who were out there for seventeen hours without inflicting a single wound on a single person, even though that kind of disgusting stuff was being thrown at them, and at *all* … of American Society.

Howard K. Smith   Our assistant director, who was injured at the scene, said there ought to be a different way to handle situations like that.

Buckley (*leaning forward*)   I wish she would invent it. What are we, in fact, supposed to use when they break law and order, as handed down by judges? Right to assembly is not absolute, the Supreme Court has ruled on several occasions.

Howard K. Smith   Let Mr Vidal have a chance.

Vidal   The right of assembly is in the constitution, in the Bill of Rights.

Buckley   It's not absolute; not without / consequences.

Vidal   Nothing on earth is absolute.

Buckley   It's not –

Vidal   That's right, we live in a relativist world. However, it is the law, it is the Constitution, and ... let us have no more sly comments in your capacity as enemy of the people. I was out there. There were none of the obscenities which your ear alone seems to have picked up. They were absolutely well-behaved. Then suddenly the police began –

Buckley   I was there.

Vidal   No, you said you were on the fifteenth floor, I don't believe you were there. And furthermore, the leaders of the New Left who were involved in this are talking about *revolution*. They are not talking about bloody civil war, as you would indicate.

Buckley   Yeah, yeah. All you do is violate the law –

Vidal (*voice raised*)   It is no violation of the law to freely demonstrate! They came here for free assembly. They have not been allowed to hold a demonstration in Soldier Field.

(*Growing angrier and louder.*) Instead, the police, fired up by Mayor Daley and a lot of the jingoes around here, have been roughing up everybody ... and you want to sit here and talk about (*a* **Buckley** *impression*), 'law and ooordeeer'.

Howard K. Smith   Mr Vidal, wasn't it a provocative act to try to raise the Vietcong flag in the park, in the film we just saw? Wouldn't that invite – raising a Nazi flag in World War II would have had similar consequences?

Vidal   You must realise what some of the political issues are here ...

Buckley   You are so naïve.

Vidal   There are many people in the United States who happen to believe that the United States' policy is wrong in Vietnam and the Vietcong are correct in wanting to organise their country in their own way politically.

(*Raising his voice more.*) If it is a novelty in Chicago that is too bad. I assume that the point of American democracy is you can express any point of view / you want –

Buckley   Yes, and some views have consequences –

Vidal (*waving him off*)   Shut up a minute.

Buckley   No, I won't. Some people are pro-Nazi. And the answer is that they were well-treated by people who ostracised them, and I am for ostracising people who egg on other people to shoot American marines and American soldiers. I / know you don't care ...

Vidal   As, as far as I'm concerned, the only sort of pro or crypto-Nazi I can think of is *yourself*. Failing that, I /would only say that we can't have –

Howard K. Smith (*interjecting*)   Now let, let's, let's not call names –

Buckley (*straight at him*)   Now listen you *queer*. Stop calling me a crypto-Nazi –

Howard K. Smith   Let's, let's stop calling names –

Buckley   – or I'll sock you in the Goddamn face, and you'll stay plastered.

Howard K. Smith   Gentlemen! Let's –

Vidal   Oh, Bill ...

A cacophony of cross-talk now, **Vidal** *grinning at first,* **Buckley** *leaning in closer and closer to him.*

Buckley   Let the author of *Myra Breckinridge* go back to his pornography –

Howard K. Smith   Gentlemen.

Buckley   – and stop making any allusions of Nazisms.

Howard K. Smith   I beg you.

Buckley   I was in the infantry in the last war / and fought Nazism –

Vidal   You were not in the infantry, as a matter / of fact you didn't fight in the war –

Buckley   I was in the second battalion! (*Leans back into his chair.*)

Vidal   You were not –

Howard K. Smith   Gentlemen.

Vidal   You're distorting your own military record.

Howard K. Smith   Mr Vidal – …

A moment. **Buckley** *back fully in his chair, staring out.* **Vidal** *glancing at him.*

In the studio, crew looking at one another confused.

In the producers' box, **William Sheehan** *shakes himself out of it, speaking into his mic.*

William Sheehan   Uh, um Howard, move on and, and then wrap up –

(*Then off mic.*) My God …

Howard K. Smith   Wasn't it a provocative (*clear his throat*), a provocative act to pull down an American flag and put up a Vietcong flag even if you disagree with what the United States is doing?

Vidal   It is *not* a provocative act. You have every right in this country to take any position you want to take because we are guaranteed freedom of speech. We've just listened to a –

Buckley   Certain – certain acts … .

Vidal (*raising his voice over him*)   – a rather grotesque example of it.

Buckley   Certain acts that are lawful are – … (*trying to recover himself enough to finish*), are nevertheless provocative. I think this is something a lot of people don't understand, that the reason we succeed as a society is we *exclude* certain things. We exclude genocide. We exclude class hatred – we ought to exclude it.

Howard K. Smith   Mr Vidal?

Vidal *is almost hesitant now, the adrenalin gone …*

Vidal   What more to say? There are many acts which provoke. What are we doing fighting in Vietnam if you cannot freely express yourself on the streets of Chicago.

Howard K. Smith   I think we have run out of time, and I thank you very much for the discussion. There was a little more heat and a little less light than usual, but it was still very worth hearing.

That is all from Chicago. Goodnight.

The studio lights snap out.

William Sheehan   … And, we're out!

Buckley *tries to remove his mic pack in a panic.*

Howard K. Smith *leaves his desk, approaching producer* **William Sheehan**.

Howard K. Smith   Sheehan, is – is he allowed to say that?

William Sheehan   I mean, we were live, and he did say it. So …

Some phones around him start to ring.

William Sheehan   Ah shit, *shit*. (*Answers one.*) Yes?!

Buckley (*to an assistant*)   Please, can you get this off me? Please?

Elmer Lower   What in Jesus goddamn Christ?!

William Sheehan   Boss, we know, we know, look –

Elmer Lower   The phone calls I'm getting –

William Sheehan   Yeah ok, some, some sponsors are freaking out a bit, but –

Elmer Lower   Spons – … forget them, my own mother just called! Furious!

Vidal   Well. We certainly gave them their money's worth tonight.

Patricia Buckley (*entering*)   Bill?

Buckley   That was a disaster.

How in God's name did this happen?

Lights!

Epilogue

Against the darkness snaps up the footage from the final debate, playing back above us.

V/O The only sort of pro or crypto-Nazi I can think of is yourself. Now listen you queer. Stop calling me a crypto-Nazi or I'll sock you in the goddamn face and you'll stay plastered.

Our characters turn to watch it, or one by one come back to the soundstage, staring up …

They snap off, and we find …

A young media analyst, **Brooke Gladstone**, *watching them from the gallery.*

Brooke Gladstone   Well. There you go.

I'm sat here, just as you are, watching decades later. Trying to make sense of it all. Trying to understand.

An older **Howard K. Smith** *joins her. She stands to shake his hand, introducing herself, notepad out.*

Brooke Gladstone   Brooke Gladstone. I'm a media analyst, hi. Mr Smith, that must have been quite the night for you?

Howard K. Smith   Quite the night? I was told the network heads – forgive me – 'shat' themselves. That kind of – 'hate', so openly displayed on live television … ?

Until, that is – the ratings came in. And –

We find – **Elmer** *and* **George** *at ABC. Popping champagne, or equivalent. Cheering.* **Howard** *joins them, less certainly.*

Elmer Lower   Ten million homes! Ten million! We've beaten CBS, *and* NBC, can you believe it. Howard, you did it!

Howard K. Smith   What did I do, Elmer? We wanted 'conversation'. They were just – they were just screaming, at one another.

Elmer Lower   Come on, celebrate. From third, to first! We're Number One!

Elmer Lower/George (*following his lead*)   We're Number One!

Howard K. Smith   *We're* Number One.

They depart.

David Brinkley   From then on, guest commentators became the norm on every network. Mr Pro versus Mrs Con, put them together, fire them up, get them going.

Elmer Lower (*yelling over, as he departs*)   Oh, just different points of view, having it out.

These all clear, as we find –

Gore Vidal *and* **William F. Buckley**, *facing away from one another, at their own respective views.*

Patricia *and* **Howard** *step forward between them. Maybe there is sunlight, and the sounds of the sea …*

Patricia Buckley   Poor Bill, I know how much he regretted it, deep down. I saw it … in the years we spent together at home, overlooking the calm waters in Connecticut.

Howard Austen   And Gore, perched high above the sea at Ravello, Italy. Regretting absolutely nothing.

They never saw one another again. An arrangement that suited them both.

Patricia Buckley   Oh please. They went on, for the rest of their lives, obsessing and utterly loathing each other, in the way that only two men so similar can.

Buckley (*sighs a heavy sigh*)   I never watched the debates again. Far too busy, much too much to do.

In Ravello, **Matt** *and* **James Baldwin** *are joining* **Howard** *and* **Vidal**.

Matt   Gore has a VHS copy of the debates. He watches them constantly.

Vidal   You snitch!

And why the hell shouldn't I? I won, after all.

Howard Austen   Did you? I mean, Gore, I adore you. I'm just saying. Who won that election? Nixon. Then we got Reagan, which – (*at* **Buckley**) – to be fair this man, Bill practically invented. Conservatism, taken root in America.

(*To* **Brooke**.) I mean, you've seen them. Are they something, or nothing?

Brooke Gladstone   Well. In terms of 'language', yelling the word queer live on television certainly broke an unbreakable taboo.

(*From her notes*.) After that, on American television we had –
well, a 'motherfucker' a year later, on Dick Cavett's show. We
waited eight years for a 'dirty bastard' by a Sex Pistol in the
UK.

Vidal   Is that so. (*Then*:) How long did we have to wait for
a cunt?

Brooke Gladstone   1999.

Buckley *sighs in his world, disappointed.*

Brooke Gladstone   For me, watching them again … they
remind me of a time when television was still a public
square, where we all gathered together. More and more,
we're polarised into these communities of concern. Living in
our own separate realities. What can I say? It makes us less
of a nation.

Patricia Buckley   It was Bill who died first.

Buckley (*turning to* **Patricia**)   Only a matter of months after
you, Ducky. There didn't seem much point hanging around.

And I was – just so tired, of life.

Howard Austen   I'm afraid it gave Gore a great amount of
pleasure, to outlive Bill.

The problem was that Gore needed things to fight against,
and without Bill …

Vidal   … And without you.

Howard Austen (*smile, hand on his face*)   It all went by so
quickly, didn't it.

Vidal   Of course it did. We were too happy.

Howard Austen   Write about that. (*At the audience*.)
Tell them how quickly it goes.

Vidal   Oh, they know. They just won't do anything about
it …

(*Seeing* **James**.) What about you, James? Is Howard right, do I thrive off hating my enemies?

James Baldwin (*swirls his drink*)   All I know is … whatever the hate, wherever it comes from, it will always eventually destroy the one hating. It is an immutable law.

(*As he's leaving.*) Be happy. Gore. Be good, and be happy …

He leaves, **Vidal** *watching.*

Brooke Gladstone   What I don't understand is that you *did* see each other again.

Vidal/Buckley   We did not.

Brooke Gladstone   You keep saying that, and you wrote that, but the memory shifts to suit the narrative, it's not the reality, the reality is there was one more debate, after that famous one that night, in Chicago?

Vidal   Really? I don't recall. (*Then at* **Buckley**.) Do you?

Buckley *is handed a clipboard, as they both sceptically retake their positions in their seats.*

They are tentative. More considered. More aware that their time on stage is coming to an end …

Brooke Gladstone   What might you actually say to one another, I wonder, off camera if you could. Not performing, this time. Just talking. Like a true debate should be.

The cameras begin to roll, studio lights up –

Buckley   … Sure. I think what I'd like to say …

The studio lights cut out.

They are alone. Just them. Together. There is a different, more intimate quality to their conversation, here …

Buckley   I should like to *ask* … do you really loathe it all, so much. The America that gave you everything, celebrates you, *accepts* you?

Vidal   Hah, does it indeed. They wouldn't elect me, remember.

And why not? Do you think if I'd tried to be more ... (*sighs*) 'likeable'. Easy going, like you? Like –

Buckley   Bobby? ... (*shrugs*) I mean, you clearly – attract people, their curiosity. But then they leave, at the end of the party, the end of the night, with a waspish anecdote from 'Gore Vidal', and where are you? Left alone.

Vidal   No, never alone –

Buckley   Never on your own. But always alone. Which / I know you revel in –

Vidal   Now Bill, I know it must be lonely for *you* up on your moral high ground but –

Buckley   – yah, I know how your side always revel in sneering at those of us with, with what, traditional values, a conventional family? I know you think the way you live *your* lives is oh so 'brave'; well you know what real bravery is? Loving someone, so completely.

Aware perhaps of where **Patricia** *was.*

Being committed to a person, so entirely, that losing them would break you. And you know that, don't you, 'Gore' – whoever the hell that is – which is why you can't commit to anything. To a person you can't leave; a home you can't move from; yeah I know, the Left's view of these small town people, 'how pathetic'. Pride in their country, 'how naïve'. Having a God, to believe in, 'imagine' ... (*Perhaps looking up, briefly.*)

Have you ever believed in anything that much? Apart from yourself. No –

Vidal   Yes.

Buckley   Sure.

Vidal   Once, yes. And that once was enough ...

I thought of him as my twin, actually. As close as two things can be, from almost our first breath, one half of the same whole, always there ...

Until he was killed. In the War. One of those things you love so much, and / I find so –

Buckley   I don't love war.

Vidal   All that I was not, he was. And all that he was not, I was. The two of us would have been pretty good, rolled into one, actually. But alas ...

A moment.

But you see the thing is, Billy Buckley, you ...

Buckley *squirms irritated*. And **Vidal** *regrets, a little*.

Vidal   ... William. You want to preserve traditional structures, because these structures traditionally benefit you. You talk of fear, but isn't that where all your politics come from, isn't that what Conservatism is, being utterly terrified of 'change'.

Buckley   Ok –

Vidal   – of the world altering, into something you don't recognise and can't control.

Buckley   Mr / Vidal, what –

Vidal   And it's why you can't ever forgive yourself for exploding at me, live on television, isn't it. It tears you utterly apart. The one single time you *weren't* in 'control' ...

Buckley *(sighs)*   ... I ...

Vidal   ... of yourself, your emotions, your natural instincts on full display. It's why you're happiest, I think, when you sail, out in the open water, away from the world.

Vidal   In front of the world, you called me a queer.

Buckley *(pause)*   You called me a Nazi.

They look at one another. And nod.

Buckley   …

Vidal   In my more generous moments, I'm almost sorry.

Only very, very occasionally.

And you?

The lights snap back up, 'on air'.

Howard K. Smith   Mr Buckley?

The two get their bearings again.

Buckley   Uh … what does concern me greatly, is of the whole notion of what it is we need to keep 'civic union' working.

Howard K. Smith   Mr Vidal?

Vidal   … I think it is quite serious. I see a great split coming. And I … I would agree, with Mr Buckley … to that extent.

Buckley *looks, trying to hide his surprise.* **Vidal** *clears his throat and sits up a little.*

Vidal   And, um. No reflection Mr Smith, but I do now think such debates are absolute nonsense. The way they are set up, there is almost no interchange of ideas.

Buckley *might find himself looking at* **Vidal** *now, listening.*

Vidal   Very little, even, of authentic personality. There's also the terrible thing about this medium, that hardly anyone *listens*. They sort of get an impression of somebody and they think they figure out just what he's like, by seeing him on television.

Buckley *makes notes.*

This would mean that you might have the most disastrous man in the country who just so happened to be an entertaining television performer ... and he could beat a virtuous person of no telegenic charm.

The whole thing has been taken over, (*pointing*) by this camera. Does television run America? There is an implicit conflict of interest, between that which is highly viewable, and that which is highly illuminating.

So, all in all I hate to suddenly come out against the idea of 'debates' in our lives, but the way they are now set up, on television ... honestly I don't think I'd even bother to watch *this* one.

Howard K. Smith *considers this. Sliding his own notes to one side.*

Howard K. Smith   Well, what ... what qualities, then, if you don't believe in debates ... What would you suggest that people judge candidates by? Mr Buckley?

Buckley   Uh. Uh, here is what I would say. I would say ... that we live in an age, when people wander around pursuing their own private vision, irrespective of whether or not it gets in the way of other people.

So, one thing we ought to attempt is to show how that moral arrogance which characterises most units of our society today ... are going to make democracy – impossible.

Howard K. Smith   Thank you very much, gentlemen. We're going to have many more pressing issues, and events, coming up this year, and indeed beyond. I wish you were here, to comment on them. But, in your absence ... we shall try to do our best.

The screens begin to crackle with static, as the lights begin to fade. Blackout.